Antony Réal

The Story of the Stick in All Ages and Lands

A philosophical history and lively chronicle of the stick as the friend and the foe of

man

Antony Réal

The Story of the Stick in All Ages and Lands
A philosophical history and lively chronicle of the stick as the friend and the foe of man

ISBN/EAN: 9783337070786

Printed in Europe, USA, Canada, Australia, Japan

Cover: Foto ©ninafisch / pixelio.de

More available books at **www.hansebooks.com**

THE STORY OF THE STICK

In All Ages and Lands

*A Philosophical History and Lively Chronicle of the Stick as the
Friend and the Foe of Man. Its Uses and Abuses.
As Sceptre and as Crook. As the Warrior's
Weapon and the Wizard's Wand. As
Stay, as Stimulus, and as Scourge*

TRANSLATED AND ADAPTED FROM THE FRENCH

OF

ANTONY RÉAL
(FERNAND MICHEL)

A NEW EDITION

WITH AN INTRODUCTORY LETTER

By WILLIAM HENRY HURLBERT

Illustrations by Alfred Thompson

NEW YORK
J. W. BOUTON, 8 WEST 28TH STREET
1892

M. ANTONY RÉAL

AND

HIS "STORY OF THE STICK."

A PREFATORY LETTER TO THE PUBLISHER.

MY DEAR MR. BOUTON:

When you asked my advice, a good many years ago, as to publishing your translation of the "Story of the Stick," I answered you like a Delphic oracle, as you said, that because the book was well worth translating you had better let it alone. Of course you had made up your mind to publish the book before you asked any advice upon it—and that you were right from your own point of view to disregard my friendly counsel may be inferred from the fact that you now mean to repeat the experiment, in a more costly fashion—with the help of a clever and skilful artist, whose pencil M. Antony Réal would certainly have called a "civilizing stick."

Nevertheless, if you were right from your own point of view to disregard my counsel, I was right to give it.

It is not quite just to say, with the Italians, that every translator is a traitor. But the things in a book which make it best worth translating are in their nature untranslatable; and the books which we call good translations are not translations at all. Fair white plumes

"danced in the eye" of Lord Berners when he read
Froissart; and he made an English Froissart as good as,
but quite other than the French.   Sir Thomas Urquhart
"shook and laughed in Rabelais' easy chair;" and he
put his delight into an alleged version of certain books
of the Curé of Meudon which has become an English
classic.   We owe a great debt to him, and to his ad-
mirers and followers, the quaint old Norman "city
merchant" Motteux, and Ozell.   But Rabelais remains
and to the end of time will remain untranslated and
untranslatable.   I have always held it an abomination
to interlard English writing or English talk with
foreign phrases or words.   But if one is ever obliged (as
may possibly happen) to cite a foreign author, it is not
only an abomination, but the abomination of desolation,
to cite him in any language but his own.   Years ago,
during a visit to England, I spent a summer afternoon
with that delightful Spanish scholar and ideal Tory,
Richard Ford, who thought Wellington and Waterloo
the final cause of Spain and the Spaniards.   It was at a
charming villa, long since swept away in the maëlstrom
of modern improvements, near Wimbledon; and at his
request I made Mr. Ford a sherry cobbler, of which in
those days Englishmen had heard only from globetrotters
and wandering Yankees, as the homekeeping dames of
the Middle Ages heard of Persian sherbets from stray
pilgrims and returned Crusaders.   While we talked, one
of the company quoted a proverb as from the lips of
Sancho Panza.   "Sancho Panza never said anything of
the sort," replied Mr. Ford, "Motteux said it."   He
then quoted the proverb as Cervantes put it into the

mouth of Sancho—and holding up against the sun his tumbler wherein the broken ice made shimmers of light through the deep amber liquid, he went on : " this is a delectable drink which our American friend has concocted for us, and there is an undeniable flavor in it of sherry—but Motteux is no more like Cervantes than this drink is like a glass of Amontillado.''

Edward Fitzgerald has given the English-using world an immortal poem. But, without being a Sir William Jones, one need only look through what we are assured is the careful and exact French prose version of the Rubáiyát of Omar Khayyám to see (what we might be sure of without taking the trouble) that talk about a ''good translation '' had better be left by men of common sense to Bottom, in the " Midsummer Night's Dream,'' or to Tartarin de Tarascon, masquerading on the tower of his indiscreet neighbor, the Muezzin of Algiers. Who can say how much of its dismal history of religious strife Christendom owes to the popular canonization of vulgate versions of the Christian Scriptures, authorized and unauthorized, revised and unrevised?

But this leads to thoughts which transcend my theme. What I have said I have said only as my excuse for saying nothing about your translation of the " Story of the Stick,'' which indeed I have neither read (though I treasure the copy you were so kind as to send me) nor intend to read.   And having said this I ought to say something of the original and of its author.

M. Antony Réal is no more M. Antony Réal than '' Arrigo Beyle '' was Arrigo Beyle.   Whether it is excess of modesty or excess of vanity which leads and has led so many writers to re-baptize themselves is a curious question which may be left to the curious. As a matter of fact, M. Antony Réal, outside of the booksellers' shops, lived and moved and had his being as M. François-Fortuné Fernand-Michel. He came of a Provençal stock, and was born in the pretty and prosperous Southern town of Solliès-Pont, in the picturesque department of the Var. He was not born a poet, and it is to be said to his credit that he soon gave up trying to make himself one. But he was born with the poetic instincts of the Provençal, and these give a certain life and color to all the work he did in the way of his profession as a man of letters—as, for example, to his history of the life and labors of Mgr. Faraud, the French missionary bishop of Anémour among the aborigines of the "great lone land" in North America. How many readers of "Sappho" or "Jack" can imagine Alphonse Daudet composing a chronicle of the wonderful work done among the negroes of Northern Africa by the missionary Zouaves? And yet undoubtedly Alphonse Daudet could make such a chronicle not only as interesting as any of his own romances, but at least as true to the spirit and the life of that extraordinary enterprise as the authentic narrative which we have of it from one of the best of Catholics and of men. There is a dose —not often a large dose perhaps—but a dose of the genius of Daudet in every clever man of letters who brings with him to Paris and to the long tables of the Bibliothèque Nationale, the remembered perfumes of the lavender and the rosemary, and the noontide shimmer of the South of France.

Any writer as clever as M. Antony Réal might have made the " Story of the Stick " entertaining had he written it under Louis XV. or during the Second Empire, as entertaining and—as unprofitable—as M. Octave Uzanne has made the " Story of the Fan " and the " Story of the Umbrella." But M. Antony Réal grew to manhood in a region haunted with memories of battle and bloodshed from the days of Caius Marius to the days of Consul Casaulx and Libertat, and from the days of Henry IV. to the days of the *Marseillaise;* and wrote his book after Jules Favre and Thiers had swallowed the bitter cup put to their lips by the inexorable German Chancellor, and writing then the story he has made it more than entertaining. For him the " Story of the Stick " is the " Story of Civilization," and the " Story of Civilization " as illustrated by the " armed peace " which ever since France was felled by Germany has brooded over Europe like a nightmare. For him the stick is at once the distinguishing prerogative and the primeval curse of man. It is the instrument at once and the symbol of that eternal strife which Hobbes declared to be the natural state of man. About it is rolled the scroll of human history from the murder of Abel to the bombardment of Paris. It is to him as it was to the author of Atalanta in Calydon.

> " Wrought for a staff, wrought for a rod
> The bitter jealousy of God."

This is the keynote of his book, and this lifts it out of or rather sets it apart from the class of contributions to " Notes and Queries," to which at the first glance it may

seem to belong.   In a social edifice in which ties are giving way and beams and rafters audibly cracking this gives
perhaps a certain tonic value to the book if the reader
chooses so to read it.   In our age of over-legislation, when
it is fashionable to cry aloud that " force is no remedy ; "
and when persons not in straight-jackets profess
seriously to believe that a million flygobblers must
necessarily be wiser than a single Solomon, it may be
profitable for others than Frenchmen to remember
that the lush and prolific legislation of the first French
Republic found a remedy in the force of the first
Napoleon.   If ordinances and decrees would have done
the work of France in 1871, the Government of the
National Defence would have raised the Siege of Paris
and kept the frontier of the Rhine.   But, as M. Antony
Réal sadly sees, the stick forever asserts itself as the
final argument not of kings alone but of republics.
What but the stick translated 1776 into 1783, and the
rebellious '' Mr Washington '' into the First President
of the United States ?

Was it the evasive and non-committal Treaty of
Ghent, or the vigorous gloss put upon that Treaty after
it was signed and before it was ratified, by a stick of
'' old hickory,'' at New Orleans, in January, 1815,
which saved Louisiana, and the Mississippi, and the
destinies of America ?

In the battle-royal of two ripe civilizations as in the
duel of two primeval savages the stoutest cudgel
wielded by the strongest arm must win.

M. Antony Réal, as a man of letters, makes much of
the peaceful, social, domestic, stimulating and ceremonial

aspects of the stick.   He tells many good stories of the
crosier and the sceptre ; he is as wise as Erasmus about
the ferule if not as learned as Buckle about the birch.
He has nothing to say, oddly enough, of the drumsticks
which tradition tells us were first wielded by the
Cimbri and the Teutons in his own native region ;
and he is silent about the cane of M. de Balzac,
but he is eloquent over the cudgel which disci-
plined Voltaire, and over the riding-whip with which
Louis XIV. dismissed his refractory estates of the realm.
But his heart is obviously in the heart of his theme ; and
the simple moral of his " story " is that the power to arm
himself given by the Creator to Man alone among the
animals means, as it has meant from the beginning, that
Right must rest absolutely upon Might.   A melancholy
moral certainly.   But as certainly, in the odious jargon
of our time, very "*fin de siècle.*"   If we are to live by
the light of science alone, who can possibly gainsay it ?
Is it not the doctrine of the " survival of the fittest "
done into Ethics and into plain English ?

There is an old French story not told, as I remember,
by M. Antony Réal, of Maître Guillaume, the official
" fool " or licensed wit who at the court of Francis I.
represented what we in this age more or less sincerely
pretend to love and worship as the freedom of the Press.
Maître Guillaume was a good democrat.   He used to
say that while God was making the angels the Devil took
. the opportunity to make courtiers and menials.   He
went about the Louvre with a stout short " locust "
under his robe which he called his " oysel," and it was
his wont whenever he met a particularly smart page or

lackey to thwack him soundly " on sight," at the same time calling out lustily himself for help.   M. Antony Réal is less cynical and perhaps less honest with the conquerors of his country.   He exalts the stick which holds the pen of civilized France above the stick which, being a sword in the grasp of Von Moltke, became a sceptre in the hand of the Emperor William.   If he had troubled himself with English literature, he would probably have bidden the proud Teutons remember that :

> " In the hands of men entirely great,
>   The pen is mightier than the sword."

No doubt, so say we all of us.   But in this as in other matters the " bearings of an observation lies in the applications of it."   When Von Moltke held the sword, Victor Hugo of course was the man " entirely great."   But when the first Napoleon held the sword the man entirely great bore the name of Goethe.   And so you will find that our excellent M. Antony Réal, writing on the morrow of the election of Marshal McMahon to the Presidency, utters something very like a profane hope that the penholder of " civilized France " may give place to that traditional bâton which every soldier of the first Empire was supposed to carry at the bottom of his knapsack !

Do I blame him for this ?   Not a bit of it.   It only shows his logic to be in his heart rather than in his head—and perhaps that is the safer place in which any man can keep his logic.

Faithfully yours,

WM. HENRY HURLBERT.

INTRODUCTION.

" THE story of the Stick," says M. Antony Real,
the author of the French work, which with some
alterations and additions we here present to the
reader, " is the story of civilization." In a certain
sense this is undoubtedly true, when the first wild
man of the woods broke off the bough of a tree and
fashioned it into a stick, he unconsciously began the
first drama of human history. Alone among all the
animals, man was capable of this simple act. In
performing it what a miracle he wrought. The lion
was fiercer and vastly more powerful than he; the
elephant, infinitely his superior in strength, was
scarcely his inferior in sagacity; the horse, as sus-
ceptible almost as himself of training, was beyond
measure swifter. But all other creatures on the
earth were limited, fatally and forever, by their
organization to the resources of their natural constitution. Man alone was capable of reinforcing
his material abilities by the exercise of his mental
faculties. The first man who armed himself pre-
figured all the magnificent subsequent developments
of human art and of human science.

As the thoughtful and judicious reader of this
book will perceive, before he lays it down, the sym-

bolisms of the stick are not less instructive than its direct services. Rod, scourge, sceptre : here a glittering crosier in the hands of a St. Ambrose, it waves back imperial Theodoric from the sacred threshold of the Supreme Church ; there a quivering lissom birch in the fairy grasp of a Marquise de St. Valéry, it startles the high noon of the 19th century with passionate echoes from the wild Mœnad midnight of antiquity.

The world is not yet ripe for the full truth in regard to any of the deeper and more permanent facts and forces of its own strange history. There are many things still, and those not the least vital in their value to the fearless student of humanity which must be told, if told at all, " darkly and in parables." It would have been impossible for us to tell the story of the stick worthily without touching upon episodes concerning which it is equally difficult to speak and to be silent. We have dealt with these, we trust, without widely vailing the crest of science on the one hand, or indiscreetly startling the modesty of nature upon the other.

TABLE OF CONTENTS.

BOOK FIRST.

The Origin of the Stick.

BOOK FOURTH.

Uses and Customs of the Stick.

Chapter I.

THE

STORY OF THE STICK

BOOK FIRST.

THE ORIGIN OF THE STICK.

CHAPTER I.

LEGENDARY STICKS.

The Legend of Adam's Stick.—The Legend of the Rod of Moses.—The Legend of Aaron's Rod.

HE stick is as old as the world ; it dates from the first tree ; the part it has played through the lapse of ages began with the first man.

When Adam had lost his innocence, and with it his original strength, God, that he might not fall a prey to the animals over which he had made him king, determined to give him a means of defense against them, which should be at the same time a material symbol of his authority on the earth—so he gave him a stick.

1

You ask how we know this. We are told it in three legends: the legend of Adam's stick, the legend of the rod of Moses, and the legend of Aaron's rod.

THE LEGEND OF ADAM'S STICK.

When God had created Adam he made him lord of the earth, and king over all the animals, and the animals were docile, and obeyed him. But on the day when he revolted against his Maker by eating the forbidden fruit, the animals, in their turn, revolted against him, and ceased to obey him.

In his extremity Adam called on the Lord for help, and the Lord answered:

"Since thou hast not known how to rule over the good, reign over the bad; since thou hast not known how to make thyself loved, make thyself feared."

"But, Lord, how shall I make myself feared by ferocious beasts that threaten to destroy me? How shall I be able to reign as thou has commanded, if they refuse to obey me?"

And the Lord answered:

"Take a branch from the nearest tree, and make of it a weapon, and strike with it the first animal that shall refuse to obey thee."

THE STICK AS SOVEREIGN—ADAM AND THE ANIMALS.

Adam seized the branch, the leaves fell from it of their own accord, and he found himself furnished with a stick proportioned to his height.

When the animals saw this weapon in the hands of the man, they were seized with an instinctive fear mingled with wonder, and they did not dare to attack him. A lion alone, bolder than the rest, leaped upon him to devour him; but Adam, who stood upon his guard, swift as lightning whirled his stick, and felled him to the earth with a single blow! At this sight the terror of the other animals was so great that they approached him trembling, and in token of their submission licked the stick that he held in his hand.

From this moment, adds the legend, Adam regained his empire, and the animals acknowledged him for their king.

The stick became one of the chief prerogatives granted to man. He alone of all created beings had the intelligence to see its utility, the right to bear it, and the power to avail himself of it.*

* Certain philosophers have asserted that the ape knows the use of the stick, and try to prove by this that man is only a developed ourang-outang. This proof would be conclusive if the statement were true, but we know that this interesting animal acts solely from imitation.

THE LEGEND OF THE ROD OF MOSES.

Moses knowing that his brethren, the children of Israel, were groaning under the yoke of Pharaoh, had dared to declare his hatred for the enemies of his people; but his patriotism gained him nothing but the anger of the king. He was obliged to flee from Egypt, and to exile himself on the other side of the Red Sea, in the land of Median.

At this time Moses was forty years old. One day, as he was resting under a fig-tree, near a well, he saw coming towards him, with her jug in her hand, a young girl whom he knew for the daughter of Juthro, a priest of Midian.

This young girl was named Zipporah.

And finding her beautiful, he asked her to be his wife.

"My lord," answered the young Midianite, "what you ask is full of danger for yourself. Do you not know that my father is a magician, and that he requires every man who asks for one of his daughters in marriage to bring him a stick which he has planted in his garden, and that up to this time every man who has touched the stick has perished?"

"And where did Jethro get this stick?" asked Moses.

Zipporah replied: "God made this stick in the beginning of the world, and gave it to Adam; Adam left it to Enoch; Enoch to Noah; Noah to Shem; Shem to Abraham; Abraham to Isaac; Isaac to Jacob, who brought it into Egypt and gave it to Joseph. Joseph dead, the Egyptians pillaged his house, found it, and carried it to Pharaoh's palace. My father at that time was one of the principal magicians of the court: he no sooner saw the stick than he divined its celestial origin, and carried it to his own house. As soon as he arrived there he hastened to plant it in his garden, saying, 'Let no one touch thee and live, unless he be the chosen one of God.'"

In spite of these words of the young Midianite, Moses, moved by a divine impulse, went to seek Jethro, and asked for Zipporah in marriage. "I will give thee my daughter," said Jethro, "if thou wilt go into my garden and bring me a stick that is planted there."

Moses went into the garden, plucked up the stick, and brought it to Jethro. The magician, surprised that Moses had not been struck with death, looked upon him as a false prophet, who would bring destruction upon Israel. In this be-
1*

lief he caused him to be thrown into a pit that
he might die of hunger.   But Zipporah brought
him food without her father's knowledge.   After
seven years Jethro looked into the pit and found
Moses in perfect health.   Then he saw that he
who had touched the stick was the chosen one
of the Most High.   He gave him his daughter
Zipporah in marriage, and entrusted him with the
care of his flocks.

Forty years after his marriage God commanded
Moses to return to Egypt, and seeing that he
hesitated to obey:

"Fear nothing," said the Lord, "for those who
wished to take thy life are dead; go, and bring
my people out of Egypt."

"But, Lord, how will Pharaoh hear me, for
thou knowest that I stammer."

"Thou shalt tell Aaron, thy brother, what I
shall command thee to do.   He shall speak for
thee, for I know that he speaks well."

The prophet then took leave of Jethro, who
gave him the stick created by God himself in the
beginning of the world.   Moses never parted
from this miraculous rod; no other person, not

even Joshua, his disciple and successor, bore it
after him. When he climbed Mount Abarim to
die there, he ordered that his rod be buried with
him.

Joshua found in the ark of the covenant the
rod of Aaron, not less miraculous than that of
Moses.

The Legend of Aaron's Rod.

The Rod of Aaron is intimately associated
with the Rod of Moses; often, indeed, the two
rods seem to be one and the same. It is not impossible that the two brothers may have had a
rod in common, which was used by one or the
other, according to the need of the moment.

At the same hour when God appeared to
Moses, he appeared also to Aaron, and giving
him a rod he said to him : " Take this, Aaron,
and let it be the instrument with which thou
shalt perform miracles—and go and meet thy
brother in the desert.'

Aaron obeyed the Lord and went.

The two brothers met on Mount Horeb, and
together they set forth to announce to the children of Israel the will of God.

A short time after, more than five hundred

thousand Israelites, stick in hand, swarmed out of Egypt under the lead of Moses and Aaron, and began their wonderful journey across the mountains and through the seas.

The two brothers performed such miracles with their sticks as Pharaoh's magicians, tried in vain to imitate. These miracles are too well-known to make it necessary for me to repeat them here.

Moses was the political chief of his people, Aaron their religious chief. The rod of Moses was the symbol of his royal power; that of Aaron the symbol of his priesthood.

And thus we shall see how, in the course of time, the rod became, in the hands of kings and priests, the emblem of human and divine authority, the symbol of spiritual and temporal power

CHAPTER II.

CONTROVERSIES ABOUT THE STICK.

The Theologians of Leyden and Amsterdam.—At what hour did Eve eat the Apple?—The Stick question.—Of what kind of wood was Adam's Stick made?—Miraculous Sticks.—The Tree of Good and Evil.—With what weapon was Abel slain?—Cain's Stick.

THE origin of the stick has long excited the curiosity of scholars. The theologians of the seventeenth century even wondered of what wood the first stick was made.

At that epoch of religious controversies the books of Moses were peculiarly the subjects of comment and discussion; there were wiseacres ready to explain the most inexplicable things in the world. Every verse in Genesis provoked a polemic; men were ready to argue about everything; they even tried to discover the exact day and hour when Adam was chased from the earthly paradise. Mr. Caillé maintained seriously, in his dissertation upon sibyls and oracles, that it was on a Friday, at precisely nine o'clock in the morning, Eve having eaten the apple at six to a minute.

As for this question of the stick, the theologians have discussed it with fury; but, happily, only with their pens.

At that time theological disputes were carried on so violently that the discussions would very likely have been settled by blows with the instrument that was the subject of it, if the disputants had happened to find themselves face to face; but one party of the combatants wrote in Leyden, the other at Amsterdam.

Now, the theologians of Leyden maintained that the stick which God gave to Adam came from an almond-tree; they proved it by Aaron's rod, which must have been of that wood, because when it was placed in the ark of the covenant, it blossomed and produced almonds. "Besides," say those who support this side of the question, " has not the same miracle been seen in modern times? Who does not know that Peter of Alcantara, when he had refused to be the confessor of Charles V., thrust his stick into the ground, and that it immediately became a flourishing fig-tree, beneath which the holy monk found a pleasant shade?"

The theologians of Amsterdam, on the other

hand, declared that Adam's stick must have been taken from the tree of knowledge of good and evil, and that our first father had even taken the very branch round which the serpent was coiled when he seduced Eve. They gave as a reason for this belief, the fact that in the hand of Moses this stick was changed into a serpent, and from a serpent back again to a stick. " Moreover," said one of them, " is not a stick a thing of good or of evil, according as we use it for a staff, or make of it an offensive weapon ? "

Other scholars proved, by reasoning quite as conclusive, that this famous stick could have been nothing else than a piece of grape-vine— witness that of Bacchus, the most ancient and the most popular of all the gods.

This grave question gave rise to another, no less grave. Controversialists are insatiable in the pursuit of truth! When we interrogate this mysterious book which tells us of the beginning of the world, one question always leads to another.

After wondering of what wood the stick of our first father was made, scholars have sought to know with what weapon Cain killed his brother Abel; and on this subject also, opinions have been divided. The scholars of Leyden referred

to the painters, who always represented the slay-
er of Abel as armed with a jaw-bone.*   But the
men of Amsterdam declared that the crime was
committed with a club. "Why," said Francis
Vossius, author of a patriotic poem printed in
1640, " why must the club of Cain be perpetuated
in the earth, and why, in the hands of kings,
should the original blood-stain reappear upon
it ? "

———

CHAPTER III.

THE DIVINITY OF THE STICK.

*The worship of the Stick.—The spear of old times.—The spear of
to-day.—The Stick of the gods.—The Stick of heroes.*

RADITION having given the stick a
celestial origin, it is not surprising
that the earliest men regarded it as
itself divine, and that, in memory of
this ancient worship, mythology put it into the
hands of gods, poets, and heroes.

---

* [That skull had a tongue in it, and could sing once : how the
knave jowls it to the ground, as if it were Cain's jaw-bone that
did the first murder !—Hamlet.]

The ancients rendered to the emblem of the gods the same homage as to the gods themselves. The sun was their first divinity, and they did not fail to give him a stick.*

The Egyptians celebrated with great pomp the " Festival of the staff of the Sun," in the early days of October. They supposed that the planet needed a support after the autumnal equinox.

The stick was more particularly revered under the name of " spear," " lance," and " pike."

In the most remote antiquity it was at first the spear—a long stick or pole, without iron or any ornament—that received divine honors. It was the attribute of the benevolent gods, and was given to nearly all the peaceful divinities. Ceres carried the spear in one hand, and an ear of corn in the other.

A stick that was particularly revered in ancient times, was that of Bacchus—the thyrsus—a bit of grape-vine, as the Jewish authors think. " Happy the land," says one of them, " where the attribute of sovereignty, instead of being a sceptre armed with a point of deadly iron, was nothing but a simple branch of that divine plant

---

* The sceptre of the sun was crowned with an eye. The eye signified forethought, prudence ; the sceptre, authority. It is thus that the ancients represent Osiris and his son Harpocrates.

2

which symbolizes the active and exhilarating power of nature."

A stick which, above all others, had a right to the adoration of mortals, was that of Mercury— the *caduceus.**

Fable tells us that Apollo gave it to Mercury, who, in his turn, gave the lyre to Apollo. If Mercury's stick was one of the most venerated of the species, it was because it was a messenger of peace.

Heros, in imitation of the gods, received this symbol of supreme power. Homer represents Idomeneus, Ajax, Hector, Patroclus, Achilles, armed with sticks in the shape of pikes. "The pike of Achilles was so strong and heavy," says the poet, "that no other Greek was able to use it." The centaur, Chiron, had cut it himself upon the top of Mount Pelion, and gave it to Peleus, that one day it might be stained with the blood of many heroes.

---

* [Here is a Greek version apt to our subject of the proverbial expression, " a hair of the dog that bit you."

" Telephus, the king of the country, opposed and repelled them," (Greeks on their way to Troy), " but was ultimately defeated, and severely wounded by Achilles. . . . Telephus, suffering from his wounds, was directed by the oracle to come to Greece and present himself to Achilles, to be healed by applying to his wounds the scrapings of the spear with which the wounds had been given · thus restored, &c."—Grote, Hist. of Greece, Vol. I.]

The sceptre of Agamemnon, preserved at Chironea, was the chief divinity of the place. It was a long rod armed with an iron point, in the form of a lance, and it was worshipped under the name of The Lance. Nevertheless, the divine rod had not a purely moral significance. Agamemnon had lent it for a short time to Ulysses, and he had used it to strike down a Greek soldier who was running away from the fight, and to perform many other acts of prowess.

This proves that this symbol of authority was principally used for service, not for show.

For many centuries the stick was the only weapon of war, while during the same time it was the only symbol of supreme power. We are therefore free to suppose that, as authority was the attribute of the strongest, he who could wield the largest club would inspire the greatest veneration, and that this veneration was due rather to the fear of his arm than to the divine origin of his weapon.

Was it not also for the sake of inspiring this salutary fear that the first kings always claimed to be descended from Hercules, and that they never showed themselves to the people unless armed with the *massue*, that is, with a great knotty stick?

In this respect the moderns bear a strong re-
semblance to the primitive people. Authority,
backed by a sword (a stick of another sort), in-
duces in us a spirit of submission which the sword
alone would produce as well.

Men have never shown that they felt a platonic
love for the stick—they have only feared it.

CHAPTER IV.

THE PRE-HISTORIC STICK.

*The stick of the age of Flint.—The stick of the descendants of.
Jabel.—The first weapon of war.—To what nation do we owe
it ?—The ravaging conquerors of old times.—Those of to-day.*

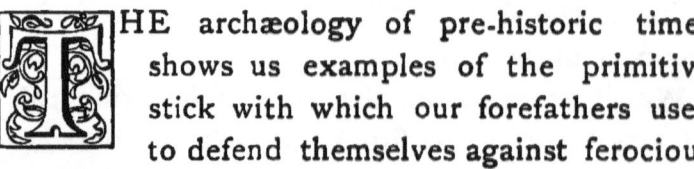HE archæology of pre-historic times
shows us examples of the primitive
stick with which our forefathers used
to defend themselves against ferocious
beasts.

A dart, formed by the bone of some animal, or
cut from the horn of the young reindeer, with a
sharpened flint, was artistically fixed in the end

of a long stick. When I say artistically, I say it deliberately. In spite of the extraordinary simplicity, and the coarseness of the labor, we see that the artist has exercised his taste as well as his skill in fixing the head solidly into the stock.

Ah! at that time life was not a torment, as it is in our day. Hunting and fishing sufficed for men's needs, and if it be true that necessity is the mother of industry, it is also true that the leisure of an easy life engenders art.

Those were happy times when the descendants of Jubal,* the first shepherd, used the stick only to guide their flocks. Tubal Cain had taught men the art of working in metals, but the descendants of Abel for a long time only used them for the pickaxe and the plough. They had not as yet thought of arming with deadly iron the peaceful staff on which they leaned while watching their flocks.

I see in imagination the first inhabitants of the earth, scattered along the banks of the great rivers, in the midst of forests and meadows, having no other fortune than their flocks, no other law than the fear of God! They worshipped God in his works. They venerated the old, and

---

* ["And Adah bare Jubal ; he was the father of such as dwell in tents, and of such as have cattle."—Gen. 4, 20.]

2*

took counsel of them. Never was any sceptre so respected as the staff of these aged men; no voice was ever listened to so attentively as was that of these living books when they taught their contemporaries the traditions of their ancestors.

Men gradually multiplied, the tribes united, cities were founded. But hatred and envy, those abominable stirrers-up of discord, slumbered as yet in the depths of the human heart—the race of Cain seemed extinct.

For how many centuries did men live in this state of calm felicity? At what time did they begin to use their sticks to slay one another? What demon was that which awakened in them the ferocious instinct that excited them one day? What nation must we charge with thus transforming the stick into a weapon of war? These are points that we can not quite determine.

Jewish writers believe that there was no war before the deluge. All that Justin tells us about Sesostris, king of Egypt, and of Tanaïs, king of the Scythians, is fable. It is Ninus, the founder of the Assyrian empire, who is accused of having brought this calamity into the world. Some authors accuse Belus, from whose name they even derive *bellum*, which word signified "war."

This Belus was the son of Nembroth, the first tyrant who made use of the stick to terrify his kind. He lived, like Ninus, in the time of Abraham, that is, three thousand years before Christ. At that time Tyre and Sidon were in the fullness of that splendor which Ezekiel long after painted for us in such glowing colors.

"Suddenly," says a historian, "an army coming out of Arabia burst into Egypt. These foreigners had for weapons sticks armed with points made of bone, and stone axes; they found a people who had no weapon but sticks, on which were written the name of their tribe, and they soon subjugated them."

These barbarians came down upon the Egyptian plains like a flock of birds of prey; they scattered desolation and death wherever they appeared, destroying everything that interfered with the establishment of their sway. They were true ravaging conquerors. The chiefs, whom Champollion-Figeæ calls "Shepherd-kings," carried a long stick armed with a lance-head as a symbol of their dignity.

Are the conquerors of to-day less worthy of the name of ravagers than those of old?

Did not the invaders of France in 1871, give to the world a still more frightful spectacle of human barbarity than that which the invaders of Egypt gave five thousand years ago ?

The golden sceptre of the German kings is not less hateful than the iron-pointed lance of the Shepherd-kings.

CHAPTER V.

THE SCEPTRE.

The sceptre.—Its origin.— The equality of the stick.— The beginning of tyranny.—The prediction of Samuel.— The first sceptre of Israel.—The first Roman sceptre.—The king-killing stick.— The stick of Tarquin.—The stick of Brutus.—Triumph of the sceptre.—The Roman Senate and the Gauls.—How long the kings lived.—How they died.—The love of the sceptre.

" HE stick is king of the world." This proverb, the meaning of which is that force reigns on the earth, concentrates in itself the whole history of the stick.

We have seen the stick force all the animals to submit themselves to Adam. We are now about to see how submissive it has made men. We will follow this instrument of executive power in the different parts it has played since the origin of society, in the hands of kings, priests, warriors, magistrates, augurs, and finally in the hands of all the delegates of authority to whom it has been assigned as an attribute, and as a symbol of command.

We will begin with the sceptre, that admirable emblem of the shepherd-kings of antiquity, the type of which was the crook.

We will not consider the sceptre in its beginning, not only because it was at first merely the peaceful attribute of the chief families among the shepherds, but because it was then called simply " a stick," and its sole distinctive mark was the name of the tribe that lived under its paternal sway. Nor will we study it at the epoch when the spirit of domination, awakening the emblem of authority, ceased to be the *hasta pura*, the pike without the iron point, and became the stick armed with iron (*le bâton ferré*). From that time the stick of the chiefs became in their hands a formidable weapon ; it took a name and ornaments peculiar to itself, and inspired fear and respect.

From the day when all sticks ceased to be equal, tyranny began.

Neither will we go back to the time when the Israelites, dissatisfied with the judges who governed them, were foolish enough to ask for a king.

"The Lord will give you a king if you insist upon having one," said the prophetic Samuel, "but take heed; his sceptre will be a heavy one; he will take your sons for his wars, your daughters for his pleasure, and your goods for his courtiers."

The Israelites insisted, and God gave them Saul, a shepherd, who at that very time was guarding his father's flocks.

The predictions of Samuel were fulfilled. As soon as the shepherd became king he levied taxes, made up a court, and waged war on his neighbors! He worthily inaugurated the power of these first anointed of the Lord, who, during long centuries, waged continual wars and spread terror, desolation, and death everywhere, until the day when the sceptre of Israel, defiled by the blood of Ishbosheth, Uriah, and Joab, was broken forever by the sceptre of Rome.

The stick, in the hands of the first kings, exerted, as it had done in the heroic times, a material force; witness Saul, who, jealous of the glory that David had gained by the defeat of Goliath, strove to kill him with a blow of the lance that served him as a sceptre. " David avoided out of his presence twice," says the book of Kings.

We see by this that the monarchs of that time did not disdain to do themselves justice, and that their sceptre was nothing less than a strong means of command, an irresistible argument for obedience.

This attribute of royalty, much more ancient than the crown, in ceasing to be the *hasta pura*, the peaceful emblem of the first patriarchs, had become a stick of war armed with iron like a lance, to which the Greeks alone gave the generic name of sceptre !

" There have gone out of Zebulon mighty ones who led their troops with the sceptre and the staff," says the book of Judges.

The office of king was not a sinecure in those days as it is now. The monarchs had no strong castles in which to shelter themselves, and crowds of servants to defend them or to execute their will. In times of war they slept under the tent as their soldiers did, and if they were attacked they defended themselves. Thus their sceptre, that is to say, their lance, never quitted their hands. We have an instance of this in the case of Saul, who had his lance at the table when he tried to strike his son Jonathan, and who **had** it also at the foot of his bed the **night** that David entered his **camp accompa**nied by Abishai.*

It was Tarquinius Priscus who first carried a sceptre in Rome, and adopted it as a royal orna-ment.   He was also the first who placed an eagle upon it.   This sceptre, fatal to the luxurious king who assumed it, seems to have been given as a warning to the kings who should come after him.

A stroke of the iron-shod stick, axe (*cognée*), deprived this monarch at once of life and scep-tre.   Servius Tullius was elected king, but after a reign of more than forty years, his daughter caused him to be assassinated, and Tarquin the Proud took possession of this sceptre, which had been twice stained with blood.

---

* From the time of Romulus, the kings carried lances or pikes in the form of sceptres.   The Frankish chiefs, who were raised upon a shield at their election carried a lance as an emblem of the sovereign power with which they were invested.   King Gou-trand gave the investiture of the kingdom of Burgundy to Childe-bert II., by putting a lance into his hand.   King Carloman, and Charlemagne, his brother, are represented in an ancient manu-script holding a rather short lance, the iron head of which is orna-mented with two curved crockets, resembling a *fleur-de-lys*, and which caused the lance to closely resemble the sceptre which was afterwards borne by the French kings.   Charlemagne had a scep-tre which was of the same length as a bishop's crook, and very little different in appearance, it seems, since a certain bishop, in the absence of the king, asked permission of the queen to use it in celebrating mass.

This bloody staff was worthy of the hands of the cruel tyrant who in his garden cut off the heads of poppies with his stick,* to intimate by such dumb show to his son Sextus, that that was the way to cut off men's heads.

At the same time the young Brutus was meditating the overthrow of royalty by offering to the oracle of Delphi a stick of elder, in which was enclosed a wand of gold. A short time after, this stick, which had been a laughing stock, had broken the sceptre of Tarquin the Proud. And the Republic was proclaimed!

The stick was no longer in the hands of the chiefs of the nations a simple piece of wood which served them as a support, or as a weapon of defense. Brass, silver, gold, and precious stones, had displaced the iron. It was no longer the symbol of material force; it represented moral force; it had ceased to be an arm; it had become an emblem, a royal ornament. This is the reason why men gave it the lofty name of "sceptre."

Cicero was the first among Latin writers who employed this Greek word.

---

* In this, Tarquin follows the example of Thrasybulus, tyrant of Miletus. This monarch, consulted by Periander as to how it were best to treat the Corinthians, led the messenger into a field of corn, and with his stick beat down the tallest stalks.

8

The sceptre was one more piece of ostentation brought into Rome together with the arts and customs of Greece. The kings and emperors placed upon it the eagle, with the word " consecratis " inscribed upon its back and around it, as a symbolic figure of the great triumph of which Tarquinius Priscus had given the first example.

Behold the triumpher clad in the royal robes, a crown of laurel upon his forehead, and in his hand an ivory sceptre, symbol of the apotheosis! He stands erect in a magnificent car. Four white horses carry him through the crowd that surges about him, to the temple of Jupiter Capitolinus; human victims, loaded with chains and marked for slaughter, accompany him. The senators precede him : hurrahs and acclamations fill the air. Why these shouts? Why these acclamations? What great service has been rendered to society by this triumphant emperor, who tomorrow, perhaps, will be numbered among the gods? This hero has caused the slaughter of five thousand men! To deserve this great ovation, a man must have slaughtered at least this number.

For centuries longer the sceptre shall thus triumph amid the acclamations of the people. Before it everything will breathe of terror and servility.

Every one will bow down, every one will prostrate himself. The royal stick shall be called a god! And the stupid crowd will applaud this impious folly!

Emperors shall become so proud, that not only will they desire to be considered as gods during life, but they will have a sceptre like their own placed in the hands of the statues of Jupiter. Their audacity shall become such that they will elevate their wives to the rank of goddesses, giving to them also the sceptre as an attribute, as Antoninus did to Faustina, to whom they even dared to set up altars!

The Roman consuls also adopted the sceptre under the name of Scipio. This was a wand of ivory, mark of their authority. The senators also carried one similar in form.

When the Gauls, under the lead of Brennus, entered Rome, they found the senators and consuls seated on their curule chairs, each one holding his wand in his hand. At this sight the barbarians paused, surprised at so much state. One among them dared to touch the beard of the senator Papirius, who struck him with his wand, and wounded him. It was the signal for a general massacre.

Never was the sceptre so majestic as then.

From Romulus to Tarquinius Superbus, seven
kings succeeded one another in Rome.   Four
were assassinated, and one died in exile.

From Augustus to Constantine there was no instance of the sceptre remaining in the same family during three generations in the direct line.
The army broke the succession at pleasure, and
few of those who wielded the sceptre died a natural death.

———

And yet the sceptre-bearers are always envied,
and certain princes have counted no sacrifice too
great that would put the fatal emblem in their
hands.   They would cheerfully cut the throats of
one half the nation for the pleasure of reigning
over the other.

———

CHAPTER VI.

THE SCEPTRE (CONTINUED).

The Sceptre of the kings of France.—The flower-de-luce.—The Sceptre of Peter the First.—The Scourge of Louis XIV.—The Sceptre upon the throne.—In the coffin.—The Sceptre is a man.— What a Sceptre is.—Superstitions.— What the Sceptre of France has become.—The peaceful Sceptres.

IN our French history we do not hear of the sceptre until the ninth century. It is not until that epoch that we see it figure as a symbol of sovereign power, with the emblems and ornaments it bears in our day. From a weapon of war it became a rod of gold curved at one end in the form of a crosier, and of the height of the king who bore it. " Its imposing length," says a critic, " was often a useful addition to the majesty of royalty."

As in ancient times, when the sticks of the chiefs were deified, the modern sceptre soon assumed in the eyes of the people an almost sacred character. It represented the authority of the king, and the king being the representative of God, obedience to the ruler of the earth must of

3*

necessity equal that due to the sovereign of heaven.

To touch or to kiss the sceptre was the highest ambition of a subject, and it was also the greatest proof of submission. The reaching of the king's arm over his sceptre was the most striking mark of his clemency.*

The oldest sceptre of the French monarchy seems to be that of Clovis. It was crowned by an eagle on a tuft of foliage. That of Dagobert was crowned with a hand holding a globe; on this globe was an eagle, and on the eagle a man on horseback. That of Philip the Fair, found at St. Denis, was still more curious—a bird emerging from an open lily.

"If I could like sceptres at all," says a thinker, "I had rather see them ornamented with the white lily, which is a symbol of hope, than with

---

* This custom was renewed by the Persians. We know that among this people, those who had the audacity to enter the king's room without being called were punished with death, if the king did not hold out to them his golden sceptre.

According to the Bible, Esther kisses the sceptre of Ahasuerus as being a symbol of mercy. Aristotle says that among the ancients the sceptre was above all a symbol of truth. That is why our first kings, in imitation of their predecessors, swore by the sceptre. It was interposed between struggling enemies. Mercury's caduceus is the sceptre which served to separate the two serpents that surround him.

that proud eagle which signifies " master of thunder."

The French kings are represented with a sceptre in one hand, and a stick in the other, because
it was thus that they appeared at public ceremonies. They intended to show by these different
sticks their readiness to punish, and their power
to reward. In the statues of the first races the
sceptre is peculiar to the kings of Paris. It was
the sign of their supremacy over the other French
kings.

From the reign of Louis X. to that of Charles
VI., the sceptre reached from the ground to the
top of the king's neck—some of them even
reached above the head, while the royal stick, on
the contrary, never reached above the bust.

This is the stick that St. Louis held in his
hand when he was rendering justice under an oak
in the *bois de Vincennes;* the hand of justice which
crowns it is his.

From the reign of Charles VII. to that of
Francis I., the sceptre and the stick were of equal
length.

It seems that the whip was, if not a symbol, at
least a prerogative of supreme power.

When Louis XIV. pronounced his famous
" L'Etat c'est moi ! ! " he held a whip in his hand,

and this whip may still be seen by the curious at the *Musée des Souverains*, where it figures most advantageously with the sceptre, the royal stick, and the hand of justice.

The hand of justice was also a sceptre of another kind, fifty centimetres long, at the end of which was an ivory handle in relief.

In the year 1679, after an astronomical discovery, the sceptre was placed in the Northern constellation. Roger, in making his astronomical charts, found that there were seventeen stars which by their position represented the royal sceptre and the hand of justice, which are the attributes of our kings. He dedicated it to Louis XIV., calling attention, in his letter of dedication, to the fact that the sceptre of justice passed the zenith of Paris, as formerly the head of Medusa passed the zenith of Greece when she fell into servitude and desolation.

His majesty the " King-Sun," as Louis was called, must have felt highly flattered to see his royal stick placed in the home of the stars.

Some medals represent the sceptres surmounted with a cross. History says that Phocas, an Eastern emperor, was the first to add the cross to his.

History also says that Rodolph, count of Augsburg, after having been elected emperor, came to Aix-la-Chapelle to be crowned. Everything was ready for the ceremony, and the crowd waited impatiently at the church. At last the monarch appeared, and placed himself on a throne.

But a strange rumor is heard. The sceptre has been forgotten.

The electors want to defer the coronation—it would be incomplete without the sceptre.

There is great anxiety among the assistants; bishops and cardinals parley—the ceremony must be postponed.

Suddenly Rodolph rises, comes down from the throne, takes a cross from the chief altar, and says as he exhibits it to the people, " Behold the sceptre of the Christian prince ! "

The crowd applauds, and the coronation takes place. As there is no sceptre, the electors swear on the cross.

Yes, the sceptre of a Christian prince should never have been anything but a simple stick surmounted with a cross, with an olive-branch for its symbol. Jesus said, " Peace to men ! " and not " War to men ! "

In his triumphal march from the prætorium to Golgotha, the sceptre of the Christ-king was a reed !

The sceptre used by the French kings at their

coronation, and which before the Revolution of
1789 was kept in the treasury of the abbey of St.
Denis, was a very long stick, crowned with a
small figure of an emperor.

The following is the description of this sceptre,
which was used for the last time at the coronation of Louis XVI., at Rheims, on the 11th of
June, 1774, a year before the American Revolution broke out, and kings and sceptres began to
fall in the market!

" . . . The archbishop took from the altar
the royal sceptre, and placed it in the king's
right hand, and then the hand of justice, which
he placed in his left hand.

"The sceptre is of enamelled gold, ornamented
with Oriental pearls ; it is about six feet in length.
Charlemagne is represented on it, in relief, with
the globe in his hand, sitting on a chair, which is
decorated with two lions and two eagles.

" The hand of justice is a stick of massive gold,
a foot and a half high, garnished with rubies and
pearls, and crowned with an ivory hand, or rather
with the horn of a unicorn ; at intervals there
were three circlets of foliage, sparkling with gar-
nets, pearls, and other precious stones."

We find at the coronation of Louis XVI. all
the customs of the old monarchy. The curious

details should be read ; they can be found in a work published in 1791, called " *Correspondance secrète de la cour de Louis XVI."*

We have shown the royal stick at the ceremony of coronation ; we will now take a look at the part it played at funerals.

After the throne, the tomb !

It was the heralds-at-arms, the official repre- sentatives and inseparable companions of the king, who played the principal part at this last act of the royal comedy.

On arriving at the church where the king is to be buried, his sceptre is placed in his tomb, and then the herald-at-arms, Grand-Master of France, placing his stick in the grave, cries three times, " *Le Roi est mort !* " "The king is dead ! "

Then taking his stick from the grave he cries three times again : " *Vive le Roi !* " "Long live the King ! "

If it were our task to write the political history of sceptres, how many of them would we find which have not abused their authority? We should see that if revolutions so often break them, it is because they have always been an ob- stacle to peace among nations, and that if this cry for liberty which stirs all hearts escapes one day from all lips, it is because sceptres which for-

merly were only given to the most virtuous and
the most courageous, are now often the property
of knaves, scoundrels, and usurpers!

Napoleon I. said, " *Le sceptre est un homme, et
cet homme c'est moi !* " " The sceptre is a man,
and I am that man."

These nine words sum up the political history
of the sceptre.

We must not forget the sceptre which figured
at the coronation of Napoleon I., in 1804, and
which was regilded expressly for that occasion.
This sceptre, which was supposed to be the imperial stick of Charlemagne, was carefully preserved at the *Musée des Souverains.* But a strange
discovery has just been made. In uncovering
the skeleton of this illustrious sceptre, it was
found to be only the vulgar stick of a chapel-
singer of the fourteenth century.

No matter how rich the ornaments which dec-
orate it, and the gold which covers it, the sceptre
is still, after all, but a simple stick!

"If you love sceptres, O kings of the earth,"
said Solomon, " love wisdom and you will reign
eternally."

But kings have not followed the wise maxims
of this sage.   They have made their knowledge
consist in dazzling with external greatness, in

keeping alive the superstition of their people, and leaving them plunged in ignorance. A certain king of the East, having beaten a man to death with his stick, made the people believe that the victim had been thunderstruck for having touched it. From that time people were allowed to believe that no one could touch the monarch's stick without dying immediately afterwards.

La Boétie says that among the Episotes the people were made to believe that their king's big toe could cure all diseases, and that the incredulous were flogged into this belief.

As soon as Vespasian became emperor, he made the people of the provinces through which he passed believe that with his imperial stick he could make the blind to see, and the lame to walk.

It was long believed in France that the holy *ampulla*, the vessel containing the oil for royal consecrations, could cure the king's evil, and it was also believed that the sceptre was a preventive against sickness.

But as reason dispelled ignorance as formerly the sun dispelled chaos, reality took the place of illusion ; the king was only a man, and the sceptre a piece of wood—like the stick of the singer of the fourteenth century, which in the hands of

4

Napoleon I. was supposed to be Charlemagne's imperial stick.

Sceptres of kings and of emperors, where are ye now ?

The sceptre of the kings was decapitated on the the 21st of January, 1793, on the Place de la Revolution.

The sceptre of the emperors fell ignominiously on the 2d of September, 1870, at Sedan.

The time will come when, among all the nations of the world, the sceptre will only exist as an object of curiosity in the cabinet of some archæologist.

I am mistaken—one sceptre will always exist ! but on a signal from that sceptre men do not arm themselves to engage in bloody strife, and the sovereign of the earth who bears it, will never draw down on himself, nor on his posterity, the curses of nations.

This sceptre is the stick of the husbandman

Homer, who in his Iliad places sceptres in the hands of gods and heroes, has not forgotten to put one in the hand of this peaceful hero of the fields, whose conquests are the harvests. "The husbandman, with a sceptre in his hands, sits among the furrows without speaking."

There is another sceptre, too, which will never

be cursed, and yet from the very beginning of the world it has exercised an absolute authority over its numerous subjects. This sceptre has had its poets and its historians, its courtiers and its flatterers; its emblem is neither a flower-de-luce, nor a globe, nor an eagle; it is only a ribbon; it is the shepherd's crook.

It was the stick which was given as for an attribute to the gods of the woods and the forests, the peaceful Fauns and the tender Sylvans.

This stick was represented by our old poets under the most graceful forms, and ornamented with ribbons of every color—precious gifts of the shepherdesses of the neighborhood. In the palmy days of bucolic literature, Florian and Mme. Deshoulières celebrated it in their verses:

> " Mes chères brebis,
> Que je le regrette !
> Sans chien, sans houlette,
> Puis-je vous garder ? "

The crook presages the sceptres. Ecclesiastes affirms their connection; God has given the sceptre to kings to rule their subjects, and to shepherds the crook to feed their flocks.

The author of the *Dictionnaire Philosophique*, writing about this verse of scripture, said: " Do shepherds still take us for turkeys?"

I would prefer these two lines of Régnard to this irreverential sarcasm of King Voltaire :

" Le sort a quelquefois, d'une chaîne secrète,
Pris plaisir d'allier le sceptre à la houlette,"

if this democratic marriage were still practicable, but kings only married shepherdesses in the blessed times when shepherds only were kings.

But even in our literature this marriage is no longer popular. Estelle became a dressmaker, and Nemourin a butcher's assistant, and the only badge of our modern shepherds is the primitive stick of the early shepherds. This stick is no longer ornamented with the traditional iron for the purpose of throwing dirt at the sheep to bring them into the fold. Dogs are entrusted with this difficult mission.

CHAPTER VII.

THE PASTORAL STICK.

The Throne and the Altar.—The spiritual Stick, and the temporal Stick.—Gregory VII.—What there is in an Egg.—Battle between the Crosier and the Sceptre.—Peace is concluded.—The Pope renounces the Crosier.—The Serf of serfs.—The two Swords.—The origin of the Crosier.—The Bishops of olden time, and those of to-day.—Warlike Crosiers.—That of Christian bishop of Mayence.—That of the bishop of Bauvais.—That of an archbishop of Sens.—The different names given to the Crosier.—The Crosier of gold, and the Crosier of wood.—The pastoral Stick in the East.—The Serpent.—Emblematic attributes.

THE pastoral stick and the royal stick have the same origin in spite of their different attributions; both received their powers from God himself. One represents the altar, the other the throne. They might be called the spiritual stick and the temporal stick.

Unfortunately for the peace of the world, both wanted to govern at once the spiritual and the temporal; bishops and kings arrogated to themselves the right of exercising this double power, and wanted to bear both the crosier and the sceptre, whence sprung up an antagonism which provoked schisms, quarrels, and bloody wars, in which

4*

the pastoral stick was nearly always victorious, for this terrible stick carried in itself a mysterious force which overthrew sceptres—excommunication —" that other stick," said Et. Pasquier, " which the heads of the church used with such liberality that it fell into contempt."

Those who wish to see how bitter this rivalry (provoked by the celebrated Hildebrand) became, should read the history of the ninth century.

Like all great rulers, Hildebrand, or rather Gregory VII., used strategy to establish his theocratic government. He showed, in a council held at Rome, a hen's egg found near St. Peter's church, on the shell of which was an image in relief of a shield on which was represented a serpent. In this prodigious egg the pontiff drew attention to the fact that the serpent was drawing his sword against the church. Was not that a warning of St. Peter, who ordered him to anathamatize the sceptre of Henry V.?

Thus from a hen's egg an antagonism arose which for centuries afflicted the world.

" Those were happy times for the church," says an historian, " when the sovereign pontiff could imperiously command kings and emperors, and when he could write to his bishops throughout all Christendom :

"'If you have the right to judge of spiritual things, why not also of temporal things? If spiritual men are flogged when necessary, why not also secular men? They think, perhaps, that the sceptre is superior to the crosier! Your priesthood is independent of princes; you are dependent upon Rome alone. The sovereign pontiff is the only master of the world.'"

These quarrels, often bloody, soon apparently ceased. The pastoral stick was proclaimed sovereign, and compelled the royal stick to submit to it. The latter humbled itself and obeyed; but this obedience was only factitious—the quarrel soon grew hotter, more violent than ever.

Simoniacal princes and dissolute priests were the powerful of the earth who were contending for the supreme power.

Gregory VII., with the very best intentions, and in spite of his great genius, could not reform the morals of his time. Priests and lords remained covetous and licentious; excommunications only perpetuated revolts, civil wars, massacres, and all those calamities were the results of one word, much more temporal than spiritual—investiture.

The deadly duel between the crosier and the sceptre was brought to a close under the pontificate of Calixtus II. in 1122.

A diet was concluded at Worms. Henry V. in order to obtain peace—and above all, fearing excommunication—not only gave up investiture by the crosier but all appointments to the benefices and suzereinty on the lands of the Roman Church. In return the pope conferred upon him the power of investing bishops and abbots with benefices by the sceptre. The pastoral and royal sticks made mutual concessions, but that was what they ought to have done at first.

It was under Gregory VII. that the name of crosier was given to the pastoral stick, and that the pope renounced it. Until then, the holy father, called more especially the first bishop of Rome, bore, like the other bishops, this emblem of episcopal authority. We find the proof of this in the history of Luitprand and in the person of Benedict. This pope, renouncing the pontificate to which he had been called without the consent of King Otho, placed his pastoral stick in the hand of Leo VIII., the legitimate pope, who broke it in the presence of the emperor, the prelates, and the people.

Gregory VII. thought, as did afterwards Innocent III., that it was beneath his dignity to bear a crosier, which confounded him with the other bishops; he even wanted the name of pope, which

was then common to all prelates, to be borne exclusively by the one at Rome ; he also wanted the
pope alone to have the right to style himself the
serf of serfs.

It was part of the policy of the universal monarchy to appear the humblest, the better to govern
the greatest.　·

Of all the emblems of the episcopacy, the
popes have retained only the ring, the spiritual
symbol of the union of the prelate with his
church.

They no longer bear the pastoral stick, but for
an emblem of their sovereign power they have two
mystic symbols more significant than the crosier
and the sceptre, more frightful weapons—they
have the two swords.

In our primitive church the symbol of episcopal
authority was only a simple stick in the form of a
T, and only intended to serve as a support, for in
those days bishops were selected from among old
men. The stick was indispensable to assist them
to walk and to support their weak knees. We learn
from history that Saint Césaire made his clerk
carry an extra one ; and it was well that he did, for
one day the good old man having mislaid the one
that he usually carried, had that of his clerk on
hand to continue his inspection.

Dom Claude Vert calls the symbols of the bishops
of that time the traveler's stick, for in those days
they did not visit their dioceses in carriages as do
those of to-day ; they went on foot, simply, modestly, like the divine Master, with the traveler's
stick in hand. They inspected their churches
very regularly, and nothing stopped them ; neither
bad roads, bad weather, nor the fatigues of a long
march.

That is why we see on old manuscripts a piece
of cloth attached to the bishop's stick—it was
used to wipe the sweat from their faces.

The pastors of those days did not style themselves My Lord, Greatness, Eminence ; they all
modestly called themselves *servant of servants.*
A simple wooden stick sufficed for these humble
apostles.

The crosier was not then, any more than the
sceptre, a purely symbolic stick. Bishops even
used it when necessary as a weapon of war.

We know that under the first race of our kings,
prelates, as well as abbés, followed the armies, and
conducted their vassals under their banners.
They were obliged to do it. In the following
centuries it was no longer obligatory, but those
who were of a warlike turn could go if they chose,
armed with their pastoral stick.

History mentions a celebrated military crosier of that time—that of Christian, bishop of Mayence. This prelate flourished in the twelfth century, when the pastoral and royal stick were no longer on very friendly terms.

Christian loved war, but he had conscientious scruples about carrying the sword on account of this passage of scripture: " They that take the sword shall perish with the sword."

After mature reflection the bishop arrived at the conclusion that the scriptures did not forbid fighting with the stick, so he had an immense crosier made with which he killed nine men at the very beginning of the contest.

Pascal II., seeing the prowess of this episcopal weapon, wrote to the one who used it so well:

" To Christian, very Christian legate of the apostolic see :—May God bless the stick which he has given you to overthrow the wicked."

Prelates have not always been so scrupulous about arms as was Christian. In 1696, the bishop of Beauvais having left the city, was in full armor made prisoner by the English. The pope hearing of it, wrote to Richard I. king of England, to upbraid him for this strange conduct, keeping a bishop—" his very dear son "—a prisoner. Richard sent the pope the bishop's cuirass with this answer:

" See if this is your dear son's dress."

At the battle of Bouvines another bishop of Beauvais, brother of Robert de Dreux, " with that same hand which gave benedictions " killed with a blow of his stick the famous count of Salisbury.

At the battle of Agincourt, Jean de Montagut, archbishop of Sens, served in the army of the Duke of Orleans. He was killed at the head of his soldiers.

The bishops of to-day understand their mission of peace better than those of old. The hand which would have held the sword would not now carry the stick. They prefer to remain in the palaces, leading quiet and holy lives, and in order to preserve peace they bless their friends, and no longer excommunicate their enemies.

Several names have been given to the emblem of abbatial and episcopal authority, that of *pedum* (crook), because being bent at the top it resembles the shepherd's crook; that of *ferula*, because it is with the ferule that the master rules his pupils.

The pastoral stick was hollow, and was also called *sambuca* (elder), the wood of the elder being hollow.

It was formerly chiefly made of cypress wood, and its crook was of bone or ivory. There are

however, examples of ancient crosiers of silver
enriched with carvings and covered with gold wire.
After the sixteenth century it was of gilded
metal, whence this rather disrespectful quatrain :

> " Au temps passé des siècles d'or,
> Crosses de bois, évêques d'or ;
> Maintenant changent les lois :
> Crosses d'or, évêques de bois."

> " In the golden age of the church, we're told,
> Crooks were of wood, and bishops of gold ;
> But things move now in a different mood,
> With crooks of gold and bishops of wood ! "

The emblematic attributes of the crosier have
not always and everywhere been the same ; formerly a head figured on them or on the globe
which crowns them, and where the crook begins
mystic expressions were engraved in Latin. On
an old crosier preserved at Amiens, and which it
is said was used by the first bishops of that
city, these words are engraved on the globe :
" *Onus non honor.*" All these crosiers had not as
modest an inscription.

In the East the pastoral stick instead of being
bent was perfectly straight. The Maronite patriarchs of Jerusalem carried straight ones. They
were crowned with a globe, or a cross, or the
letter T, which was the form of those of the Greek
patriarchs The Armenian priests at Jerusalem

5

carried a straight stick without any ornament, and
the bishops a bent one, as in the West. Some of
the crosiers of the Western bishops were crowned
by two serpent's heads looking at each other.

The serpent has been held in high esteem on
earth from the beginning of the world. The ancients bore it on their shields and helmets. Cyrus,
the conqueror of the Assyrians, made the Persians
and the Medes adopt it. Placed on their military
ensigns it became an object of worship for the
Roman soldiers—the church adopted it as a presage of victory and as an emblem of episcopal prudence. The serpent on the pastoral stick was
prudence combined with cunning.

The crosier is shaped somewhat like the *litnus
pontificus*, or pontifical stick of the augurs, which
they held in their hands when they gave their
oracles. But our crosier has many more emblematic meanings; each of its parts expresses an
idea. " *Altrare per primum medio rege pange per
imum.*" "Attract by the top, rule by the middle, punish with the point." The spiritual and
temporal attributions of the temporal stick could
not have been told in fewer words.

CHAPTER VIII.

THE PASTORAL STICK (CONTINUED).

The abbatial Crosier.—Words of St. Bernard.—The crosiered Abbots.—The ceremony of bestowing the Stick.—The quarrel of the Crosiers.—Let us not speak ill of Monasteries.—The King and the Abbeys.—The abbess of Montmartre.—Henry IV.—How the pastoral Stick is carried to-day.—The Stick of the Dean of the Cardinals at Rome.—The Singer's Stick.—The most imposing of the Sticks.

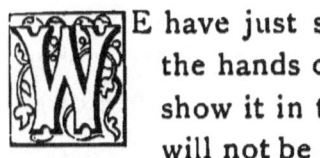E have just shown the pastoral stick in the hands of the bishops, and will now show it in the hands of the abbots. It will not be a less interesting study, and it can be pursued without wandering from our subject. As the emblem of abbatial dignity, as well as of pastoral dignity, we will always see the crosier the equal of the sceptre.

In the first place, we may say without exaggeration that the chiefs were in reality kings in their monasteries. Evangelical morality had nothing to gain from the power of abbatial crosiers ; but they co-operated in the humiliation of sceptres and the triumphs of the Roman church, so that "many sins were forgiven them."

St. Bernard thus speaks of the abbeys of his time:

"The retinue of one abbé would be sufficient for two bishops; I have seen one of them with more than sixty horses in his train. His servants carry with their baggage table-linen, goblets, ewers, sconces, portmanteaus. An abbé will hardly go four miles from home without all these things. Would no light satisfy him but that from a gold or silver candlestick? Could he not rest on bed coverings of various colors, without costly blankets from foreign countries?"

After this criticism of St. Bernard, which so well depicts the customs of the crosiered abbés, let us see how the pastoral stick was bestowed upon them.

The abbés could only perform their religious functions after having been elected by professed monks; so it was the bishops who gave them their sticks.

The chosen one, assisted by two dignitaries of the abbey, was conducted into the chancel; the bishop spoke a few words to him on the duties of his charge; then mass began, which was served by the new abbé. At the gospel the bishop gave him his benediction; and after some further ceremony he gave him the crosier, saying:

" Receive the stick of the pastoral ministry."

As soon as the stick was placed in his hand, the abbé enjoyed all sorts of prerogatives ; he could even free himself from the authority of the bishop when he pleased.

He was called the "lord abbé." He occupied the first place in everything—monks and worldlings, nobles and beggars, bowed before him. At church the priest officiated behind his chair. The censer was carried to him to receive the first grain of incense. Some kissed his hands; others begged his forgiveness!

He marched at the head of processions, stick in hand. When he intoned an anthem at church all turned towards him.

In the dormitory his bed was separate from the others, and in the refectory he had a separate table.

When during the day the bell called the monks to some exercise at which the fortunate abbé was to preside, if the hour had passed and he had not made his appearance, the bells continued to ring until his arrival. If necessary all the clocks would have been stopped in order not to make him seem tardy.

Every one who pronounced his name was compelled to bow his head, and he alone was privileged to walk with his head covered.

5*

When he returned from a journey, the monks, in their albs, went in procession and carried him his stick as though to rest him after a fatiguing march. His march, however, must have been rather light, for the lord abbé only traveled on horseback or in a carriage. He only marched in processions, and then always followed by some brother whose business it was to sing the psalms for him ; fearing that prayer might fatigue him, he recited his offices by proxy.

When he entered a city he was received by a procession. His numerous companions took off their hoods, but he kept his on.

An abbé on a journey was a king minus the name. Most of the crosiered ones were so rich that they could afford all sorts of luxuries—they had guards, gentlemen, cup-bearers, standard-bearers, a physician, an almoner to carry their money, in fact all the paraphernalia of a monarch.

An abbé of Cluny was called, *Rex Cluniacensis et militiæ princeps.* This stick governed no less than four large abbeys.

But let us be just—if the peasants around the castle were ill-treated, suffered pillage and spoila-tion, those around the monastery were helped and protected. It is only justice to the monks to say that if with one hand they plundered the rich, with the other they helped the poor. Those who were lucky enough to pass from the authority of a secular lord to that of a lord abbé felt the full truth of this proverb of the middle ages: "It is good to live under the crosier." For instead of being beaten, bought and sold like cattle, says a writer of that time, they were treated like men.

The abbés, as well as the bishops, enjoyed absolute power. Their word was law. In France, as in Germany, they were both spiritual and temporal lords; they carried the crosier, and they had a right to carry the sword.

The prelates rebelled against this prodigious sovereignty. "They have only to take from us our pastoral sticks and subject us to theirs, since they possess the churches, the lands, the castles, the tithes, the obligations of the living and the dead. The priesthood is degraded since the abbés seek our rights with insatiable ambition."

The prelates, however, were not quite justifiable in complaining. If the abbés enriched themselves by the gifts, sometimes forced, of private individuals, bishops were enriched by the liberality of the emperors and kings of France. They were created by the first prince of the empire; had the right to coin money, and even to create nobles.

And thus for centuries bishops and abbés

sometimes crossed sticks, and sometimes united to fight the sceptre.

Let us not speak ill of the crosier ; if it has sub-jugated the people, it has humbled the pride of the great ; if it has provoked wars, it has struggled with despotism ; it has ever been on the side of the feeble against the strong, of the oppressed against the oppressor.

Let us not speak ill of monasteries. If behind the pastoral stick we have seen the extravagance and laxity with which St. Bernard reproached them, they were the temples of study, the depos-itories of knowledge and learning, and an asylum always open to the unfortunate. There those who were persecuted by the civil law could shelter themselves from the violence of the feu-dal stick.

But the day came when the sceptre, envious of the wealth of the crosier, wanted to own the abbeys. The monasteries gradually lost in the hands of the profane all their former greatness. Work fled from them—nothing remained but the abuses which soon degenerated into scandals.

The emblem of abbatial dignity was no longer given to knowledge and virtue ; the king bestowed it upon his courtiers and mistresses.

This shameful traffic of the pastoral stick, begun

under Charles Martel, went on increasing from age to age until our revolution.

History mentions the abbey of St. Denis given by Louis XVI. to the princess of Conti. Her ancestor Henry IV. had done as much for the beautiful Marie de Beauvilliers, daughter of Count de St. Agnan. The place of this last celebrated crosier is here.

When Henry IV. was besieging Paris, the young Marie de Beauvilliers was abbess of Montmartre, and the pastoral stick was so becoming to her that the king having been introduced to her at Senlis fell desperately in love with her. He found her more bewitching than Marguerite of France and the Marchioness of Quercheville.

" Oh, madam, the crosier was indeed your due," said the gallant king to her.

" Sire," replied the abbess, " I hope my crosier will make my holy sisters as happy as your majesty's sceptre makes your subjects."

" Your crosier might make a king happy," said he, as he drew a little nearer the abbess. " It is a a very dangerous weapon," added he softly.

" Your majesty possesses arms that are proof against all dangers," replied Madame de Montmartre.

A few days later, the sceptre was swearing eternal love to the crosier.

We know what was the eternity of the loves of Henry IV. This one lasted four weeks.

Gabrielle d'Estrées appeared holding in her hand the sceptre of beauty, the only sceptre to which the pastoral stick had ever yielded.

To-day, according to ecclesiastical law, bishops alone have the right to carry the pastoral stick. Abbés carry it as well as bishops; but this privilege is not an ordinary right—it is a concession.

And yet the abbés of to-day are more deserving of it than were those of old.

According to the established rule, the abbé carries his stick with the crook turned in, as a sign that his jurisdiction is confined to his monastery.

The bishop turns the crook of his out, to show that his stick has jurisdiction over his whole diocese. Even outside of his diocese he carries it thus, because the Holy Ghost has established bishops over all the church of God.

The dean of the order of cardinals at Rome carries a stick as a mark of dignity. He becomes pope *ad interim*, in case of the death of the holy father. His stick is of gold, and is called *ferula apostolica*.

We have explained why, since Gregory VII., the popes no longer carry the crosier. But other reasons are given, this one among others :

Saint Peter having sent his stick to Eucherius, first bishop of Trèves, it was preserved in a church as a precious relic. After that, Saint Peter did not use a stick.

We prefer to think that the pope no longer bears this emblem of authority, because it would be contrary to the spirit of humility of him who wanted to be called the serf of serfs.

Formerly the stick figured at all the ceremonies of the church ; priests all carried one during the offices. It was intended to serve as a support, for in those days there were no pews in the chancel ; but they were not allowed to lean on them while the gospel was being sung.

There was also the chanting-stick borne by choir and procession singers. It was in the processions of the Rogations that it was most customary to use them. In the customs of many of the churches, at the ceremony of blessing the fruits of the earth, singers and penitents carried it.

It is in remembrance of the stick carried by the children of Israel when they came out of Egypt, and of their march in the desert, that we see the chanting-stick in the hands of singers and penitents.

To-day only the bishop carries the stick at church, when he officiates pontifically.

I am mistaken; another stick still figures in all the ceremonies of the church, and more than any other, enjoys an undisputed authority.

It is a serious, majestic, solemn stick; it is convinced of its own rights, vain of its function, jealous of its prerogatives, confident of its strength; it is great, but not haughty; it inspires less fear than admiration; it has an imposing address.

It is not a coarse, brutal, angry stick; on the contrary, it is courteous, complaisant, polite; it threatens oftener than its strikes; it does not like to be severe; it is a little despotic—what stick is not? But it will never be tyrannical.

It is an honest and virtuous stick, a defender of order, and a friend of peace.

It is complaisant, kind, and good. If a lady enters the church after the ceremony has commenced, it hastens to make a passage for her, and when she has made her way through the crowd, and reached her place without hindrance, how gracefully she thanks it, and then how proudly it returns to its post. We must pardon its pride—

humility is not the virtue of the stick, and if this one feels its importance, it has a good right to do so.

Have you ever seen this stately stick at the church of Notre Dame precede to the pulpit, with an imposing air, one of our great preachers? And after the sermon, how proudly he conducts him back to the chancel?

It is not the orator who charmed the audience, it is the stick. See it assist the priest to descend from the pulpit—it describes more majestic curves, striking measured blows on the sonorous flag-stones, as if it would say to the worshippers: " I made him ascend the pulpit ! "

You have guessed what stick this is—it is that of the beadle.

Against this stick the thunders of the Vatican have never resounded, and the tocsin of revolution has never rung.

BOOK SECOND

THE FEUDAL STICK.

CHAPTER I.

THE RIGHT OF THE STRONGEST.

WHILE the sceptre and the crosier were contending for the sovereign authority, the feudal stick arose threateningly on the high towers of lordly, strong castles. For the authority of kings was then dead. When Gregory VII. weakened the principle of royalty, he contributed to the establishment of an infinite number of small despotic states, out of which grew feudal anarchy, against which monarchs long contended.

Every district, every province, every village, was surrounded with walls and ditches. There was not a hill, not a steep rock on the top of which some nobleman—like a bird of prey—had not built his inaccessible den.

Despotism was there called grandeur; tyranny justice. The capricious will of a single man was the only law; the inequality of conditions a system; poverty, weakness, servitude, humbled themselves before strength and the audacity of riches, and the stultified people bent their backs to the stick.

For uninterrupted centuries, thousands of cruel petty tyrants—whose sceptre was a stick—represented lordly right, or rather lordly arbitrariness.

The feudal stick was not only an emblem, it was an active instrument of domination before which knelt serfs, villains, and peasants, as we saw the animals crouch and tremble before the stick of the first man.

Lords, on account of the great increase of peasants attached to the soil, being no longer able to govern alone, delegated their powers to officers who governed in their name.

The mission of these representatives was to keep the serfs in subjection. They had the right of life and death over them, and could punish them as they chose.

Blows were the commonest punishment, and that is, perhaps, why we see on many of the armorial bearing of old families this symbol of lordly judges.

The powers of these judges were such that when
Louis le Gros wanted to resume the authority
which his vassals had seized, he could not succeed
in doing it, either by the establishment of com-
munes, by the freeing of the serfs, or by sending
emissaries to prevent dukes, counts, and officers
of justice from ill-treating peasants.

"These officers, bearing sword and stick, were
created," says President Hénault, "to accustom
the people to the justice of the lords."

Queer justice indeed! renewed from the barbarous ages, or based on the Salic law; and which
recognized no punishment but compensation for
freemen, but which allowed slaves to be beaten
without mercy.

Vassals and suzerains alike bore stick and sword
which they only laid aside to pay homage; while
paying homage they were to unbuckle their belts
if they had one, and remove sword and stick.

Feudal society, we may say, was represented
by these two signs, "the sword and the stick."

The sword—that is, nobility—the weapon that
honors the one that it strikes.   The stick—that is,
peasantry—which dishonors whom it strikes.

This dishonor the people long bore with the un-
conscious resignation which is the mark of brutish-
ness.   The castle which overlooked the village

was long regarded as the sacred dwelling of the lord and master before whom all were compelled to kneel. Even the servants of the castle had a right to some share of this veneration.

Serfs thought they were only born for the glebe, the dungeon, the halter, and the stick. They accepted lordly justice as an article of faith.

We would have to write a long chapter to enumerate all the laws and customs relating to the justice of the stick. A serf who did not blindly obey his master was immediately bound hand and foot to a stake, as if he were going to be put to the torture, and the fewest number of blows that he received was twenty-five. For grave faults his ears were cut off, so that it was not a very rare thing to see villages in which many of the peasants were earless.

Each province had its peculiar customs in respect to punishments for each lord, and even each officer of a lord punished according to his own fancy. But the punishments were never the same for the nobles as for the serfs. No one cared for the death of the latter, while the former were never punished ; they were allowed to ill-treat peasants as much as they pleased. When a nobleman had dissipated his fortune, he, with others of his kind, went about burning villages

6*

and plundering peasants; the noble pillagers then quietly re-entered their gothic dungeons, where they continued to enjoy their feudal rights, which we may call the rights of the stick.

Woe to the serf who dared to resist or complain the least word was a capital crime. The poor fellow was even obliged in some provinces to kiss the instrument of his shame and torture.

In those days of moral and physical servitude, the great used, in order to rule the people, the devil and witches as an intellectual means, and the rope and the stick as a material means.

We must, however, record one good action of the stick. By the side of the inhuman arm that strikes, it is consoling to find a gentle hand which protects. Queen Blanche, the best of queens, and mother of Saint Louis, the best of kings, is the heroine of it.

The poverty of the inhabitants of Chateny was so great, that they had been unable to pay the canons of Notre Dame, their lords, the taille and the cense imposed upon serfs. The canons threw them into their dungeons.

Queen Blanche, hearing of this treatment, was so moved to pity that she interceded for them. She first tried gentleness, begging the canons to release the serfs under bonds.

The canons insolently replied to the merciful queen that she had no right to meddle with their temporal affairs, and that they would not release the serfs.

Incensed at this answer, the queen went to the prison followed by her guards.

"Open that door," commanded she, "or it shall be broken down!"

And, as the jailors did not reply, she struck it a hard blow with a stick which she held in her hand. At this signal the guards broke down the door, and a crowd of men, women, and children came out, throwing themselves at the feet of the good queen, and imploring her protection.

There were, however, serfs who, flogged as they were on the slightest provocation, dared to retort.

A peasant had killed a dog belonging to his lord's officer with the iron-pointed stick which he used at his work. The enraged officer wanted to have him hanged, but the peasant insisted that he had killed the dog in self-defense.

"You should have struck him with the other end of your stick," said the judge.

"Yes," replied the boor, "and so I would have done, if he had attacked me with his tail."

This answer saved the peasant's life; he was let off with the traditional bastinado.

It was no more safe formerly to speak unpleas-
ant truths to the great than it is to-day, and to
prove it we will relate what happened to Jean de
Menny.

The poet had dared to doubt the chastity of
the ladies of the nobility. Abominable! The
virgins of the court made a dreadful outcry.
They wanted an example made of him. The
wife of Philip the Fine interceded for them with
the king, who ordered that the infamous calum-
niator be arrested, stripped naked, and receive
from the hands of the outraged noble ladies as
many blows as they chose to give him.

All determined to strike many and heavy ones;
but they had reckoned without their poet's wit.
He had obtained permission of the queen to ask
one favor relating to the execution of the sentence. It was that the greatest prostitute among
the ladies might strike the first blow.

The first blow was not struck.

A day was to come when feudal despotism,
armed with the debasing instrument intended to
punish slaves, would be powerless to keep people
in a passive obedience. A day was to come when
those men who were slaves to all the caprices, all
the cruelties of the master, would begin to murmur.

THE INDIGNANT BEAUTIES, OR THE STICK FOR THE SLANDERER.

From murmurings to revolt the distance is short. The people had not become accustomed to lordly justice—they even sometimes refused to bend their backs. The nobles themselves, by their continual revolts against the royal power, had first set the example of rebellion.

Nostradamus, in his *Chronique de Provence,* gives several instances of this desire for freedom.

Pierre Rigoura, bearing the stick of justice, was accused by the people of malversation and *méchancetés* on the backs of several of the justiciables. The peasants wanted to kill him. He took refuge in a house. " That day the people had the upper hand, rascals a voice in the councils, and the wicked authority."

The house in which the unfortunate man had taken refuge was going to be burnt down by the angry populace.

" Give up your stick," cried the people.

" The lord gave it to me," replied the judge.

" Give up your stick," continued the incendiaries.

Fagots of straw and wood had already begun to burn.

" Give up your stick," was still the cry.

The justice, seeing that there was no help for it, threw his weapon out of the window, thinking it better to give up a simple stick than his own blood.

The peasants, satisfied, took the stick, and extinguished the fagots.

Having succeeded in getting the stick, they were at a loss what to do with it, so they gave it to Antoine de Cordonan.

When the people seize authority by violence they never know how to use it, and they hasten to place it in the hands of the most skillful, who never fails to use it against them.

So did Antoine de Cordonan, who, having quieted the people, gave back the stick to its owner.

These little revolts of the people gradually led to the great revolution, when they were to shake off forever the load of outrages which had overwhelmed them for so long.

The feudal stick was broken during the memorable night of the 4th of August, 1789.

CHAPTER II.

THE HERALDIC STICK.

The Stick in heraldry.—In the jousts and tournaments.—Nobility judged by the Stick.—Traditional heraldry.—The sign of bastardy.—Engraved armorial bearings.—The baton of the Bourbons.

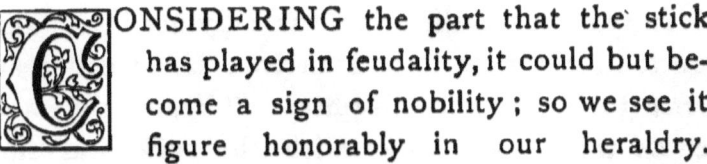ONSIDERING the part that the stick has played in feudality, it could but become a sign of nobility; so we see it figure honorably in our heraldry. Many old families, going back to the old chivalry or the crusades, bore it on their arms.

In the new armorial bearings, the stick was more particularly the sign of the office, civil or military, with which men were invested; but in the ancient ones the meaning is more in conformity with its antique usage. Thus it is not only the sign of an employment of a dignity, but it often brings to mind the jousts, the tournaments, the glorious deeds of the battle-field. It is a souvenir, a tradition.

At the exercises of the tournament, in the jousts of pleasure, the chevaliers used parade lances or rather *bâtons rompus* (broken sticks); that is, the iron point was broken or taken out. These sticks were also called courteous lances, graceful lances, innocent lances. The Romans had similar ones called *arma tresoria* (arms of amusement).

In real jousts, the stick was only used to fight on foot, but then it had an iron blade called an *estoc* (tuck), whence this phrase : " Frapper d'estoc et de taille,"—to strike with the tuck and the edge.

We must here mention a joust of the stick called *Béhouart*, which took place in several cities, especially at Amiens on the first Sunday of Lent. Although this exercise was an imitation of the pleasure jousts of the tournament, it was not always unattended with danger. The young men of the cities fought with sticks without iron points, but with which they struck close. We read in a letter of remission of 1436, quoted by Carpentier in his glossary : " On the first Sunday of Lent, those companions held *bonhours* (sticks) in their hands, with which they fought one against the other."

The law of tournaments regulated jousts with the stick.

It is said in the *Theatre d'honneur de la vraie*

chevalerie, that, "whoever strikes more than five blows with his stick loses the prize, and that whoever lets it fall also loses it."

These jousts in the tournament were presided over by heralds-at-arms, who held sticks in their hands.

It is not surprising, then, that this arm has become an honorable piece of blazonry, and that it has remained an ornament intended to perpetuate family traditions.

We read in the *Vraie Science des Armoiries :*

" The baton is well enough known, and requires no other explanation, except when it at times extends from one extremity of the shield to the other, in which case it is said to be *debruised over all* (*brochant sur le tout*).

The baton *debruised over all* is the sign of pure nobility, that which has never degenerated from ancestral virtue *(forligné)*, as they would have said in olden time.

The baton is shortened *(raccourei)*, *couped in bend* (*péri en bande*), *or couped in bend sinister* (*péri en barre*).

The obscure science of blazonry explains these different signs as follows:

The natural son of a noble, if he has been recognized, and the king has granted him letters of

7

nobility, has no right except to the shortened baton, even though his father bears it *debruised over all* in his coat-of-arms.

This contracted emblem denoting a lowered nobility, has a timid appearance at the middle of the shield.

The detracting circumstances, the mesalliances, are often indicated by the baton extending from right to left and stopping at the middle of the shield. It is then said to be " *couped in bend.*"

The baton that runs from left to right, stopping at the middle of the shield, is said to be " *couped in bend sinister*;" and it is the sign of bastardy.

The duke of Orleans, the enemy of the duke of Burgundy, bore on his banderols a knotty stick with these words, " *Je l'envie!*"

The duke of Burgundy responded by having painted on his, a plane, to signify that he would plane the knotty stick of the duke of Orleans.

Henry III. had a stick among his weapons. The day that he was assassinated a thunderbolt struck the windows of the chapel of Bourbon l'Archam-beau on which the armorial bearings of the king were represented. " Providential event," says the chronicler, " the thunderbolt broke the stick with-

out touching the three lilies, which remained in-
tact for Henry IV."

The constable Charles of Bourbon bore the
whole stick *debruised over all*, as did Francis I. and
as the elder branch of the Bourbons still bear it.

Francis of Orleans, natural son of the Marquis
de Rothebie, who was a natural son of a D'Orleans, bore the baton *couped in bend sinister*.

The duke of Main, natural son of Louis XIV.,
bore France like his father, but with the addition
of the baton *couped in bend sinister*.

Many a man of the people would not feel it an
honor to display in public the sign of his bastardy,
but great people are not expected to have much
delicacy of feeling.

From Saint Louis to Charles VII., lords and
ladies had the representation of their armorial
bearings painted or embroidered on their clothes.
The following is the description of a very curious
representation in which, among other emblems,
the baton of the Bourbons figures.

Jeanne de Bourbon, wife of Charles V., is going
to meet her mother, the duchess of Bourbon, who,
having been taken prisoner by the English, is going to be exchanged for Simon de Burle, chevalier
of the prince of Wales.

The queen carries her ensigns armorial on her

dress; on her skirt, over which lilies are scattered, is the Bourbon baton. She holds in her left hand a bird, emblem of seigniory.

The queen is accompanied by Jeanne de Bourbon, Count de la Marche, who acts as her chevalier of honor. He also is recognized by the baton of the Bourbons—but this baton is subdivided with three young lions in silver, a rebatement of Bourbon la Marche.

Then comes Maria, daughter of Charles V., about three years of age, who wears France and Bourbon. Then come six princesses of two ranks. Those of the first rank hold a dog attached to a long slip.

The first is the young duchess of Bourbon, dauphiness of Auvergne and countess of Forez, wife of Louis II. Her dress bears the baton of the Bourbons.

The train of the dress is held by the fourth lady of the first rank, who is Lady de Nedouchellé. The queen's three sisters have their dresses emblazoned with part Bourbon, and part the arms of their husbands.

Isabeau de Valois, duchess of Bourbon, mother of the queen, widow of Peter I., duke of Bourbon, wears a widow's veil, and her coat-of-arms, in which the Bourbon stick is prominent.

Before the revolution, the plainest citizen could buy titles of nobility.

The rules of blazonry having fallen into disuse, nobles were allowed to add to their arms any emblems they chose except the baton—that they could not even buy.

After the seventeenth century armorial bearings were no longer a real tradition, nor a mark of honor for the nobility. The descendants of the knights had ceased to be scrupulous in the observance of the laws of blazonry. How many have modified them to suit their whims, or according to the demands of necessity! How many more bear on their shield the baton *debruised over all*, when it should only figure there either *couped in bend sinister*, or *shortened*.

Ah, if ancestors could only return to earth, stick in hand, what a sorry figure their descendants would cut !

But we must not prolong these considerations : the science of heraldry is enshrouded in mysteries which we must not try to fathom.

It is much better for many noble families that their historical light be hid under a bushel.

7*

CHAPTER III.

MASTER AND STICK.

The title of Master.—The Stick of the Grand Valets of the court, and Grand-masters of the army.—Master in the palace.—Saint Nicholas' Stick.

ASTER! A word which the old régime used almost as much as the stick.

In their grammatical or figurative acceptation, master and stick both equally express authority.

One of these words immediately calls to mind the other. They were both destined to unite in order to command.

Master! This word reminds us of Subject. It agreed too well with the customs of feudality not to become a title with them, and this title flattered every one's vanity too much not to excite every one's ambition. In the court, in the army, in the palace, the title became a dignity, a privilege, a power.

It began at court where, by a remarkable substitution of words, the king's valets were suddenly honored with the title of master! There were no longer valets de chambre, nor stable-men, nor chief cooks—there were nothing but masters or grand valets.

Master of the wardrobe, master of the bed-chamber, master of the train. The first two valets were called grand master of France, and grand master of ceremonies.

But as if to remind the other master-valets of the court of their servile origin, the two grand masters each received a stick as an emblem of his authority.

The baton of the Grand-Master of France dates from the beginning of the monarchy. It is vir-olled with gold. The king placed it in the hands of the grand master when he was sworn.

This stick had jurisdiction over the masters of the oratory, chapel-masters, stewards, masters of the bed-chamber, &c., &c., and over many other subordinate masters.

It was the first court stick.

The stick of the grand master of ceremonies has as ancient an origin and no less power, al-though it only belonged to the second rank.

This grand master carried his symbol of com-mand at all court ceremonies. It was a stick of ordinary length, covered with black velvet. The end and the knob were of ivory.

It is to be presumed that from the day that the title of grand master was given to the domestic chiefs of the court, their office was no longer a sinecure, but an active function, and that the attributions of their sticks of command were more real than symbolic.

In the army there was the grand master of artillery, whose distinctive mark was a stick, richly ornamented like that of a marshal of France, has been made illustrious by Sully.

We must not forget the other masters of the stick, who have the honor of marching proudly at the head of battalions: the drum-master and the drum-major.

Religious and military orders, associations, brotherhoods, were governed by grand masters, or by masters bearing the stick as an emblem.

It was in the palace especially, that the title of grand master was principally honored and became generalized; lawyers, solicitors, advocates, notaries, clerks, all called themselves masters.

The chief advocate carried a stick, but it was never emblematized. Perhaps that is why the Revolution did not break it. The stick which he carried in the procession of St. Nicholas was not his own; it was that of the saint.

The title of *bâtonnier*, which is still given to the

oldest lawyers inscribed on the roll before the abolition of masterships, was given to the chiefs of different bodies, and different brotherhoods or communities.

They were called *bâtonnier* because they were selected from among the oldest men, that is, those who already needed the stick; "and they also gave them the stick," says Duconge, "to show their empire and command over all the members of the company."

To-day the title of master is no longer a privilege; it is one that every man may bear if he possesses industry, honesty, knowledge, and skill

CHAPTER IV.

THE TRUNCHEON OF THE MARSHALS OF FRANCE.

From Philip Augustus down to 1793.— The Marshal de Duras ana an epigram of Linguet.—Condé's Stick.— The flag.— The cane of Louis XIII.— The marshal's Stick as is it to-day.— The breeches of Louis XIV. and Mme. de Symeron.—How Vivonne was made marshal.— Why Crillon was not.—Crillon's Stick.— Marshal Bazaine.

HE truncheon of the marshal of France is the badge of the highest rank in the army. Scholars have never agreed on the etymology of *maréchal*, but all have agreed that originally this name signified an officer of the king's stables, whose business it was to shoe and groom horses.

When this subordinate charge became a military dignity, it is probable that the symbol of command that the king gave to his robust marshal was not a devisory emblematic stick, like that of the marshals of our day, but that it was a real stick, on the top of which, perhaps, figured a horse-shoe.

Philip I. was the first who, in 1191, gave to this stick the command of troops.

This dignity of marshal of France was then held only during the pleasure of the king. It was Francis I. who created, in 1516, the first life marshal, Gaspard de Coligny Chatillon.

Under St. Louis there was only one marshal of France ; under Francis I. there were two ; under Henry II., four ; under Francis II., five ; under Charles IX., seven ; and under Henry III., nine.

From Henry IV. the number was not limited, and when the revolution of 1793 abolished the marshalships, there were nearly five hundred truncheons on the French staff.

The example set by Scipion de Fiesque, who refused the title of marshal of France which Catharine de Medicis offered him, had not many followers. " Madam," replied he, " I have served long on land and sea, and I have always conducted myself like an honorable man, but that does not suffice to give me the right to bear the truncheon."

This stick is one of those which has always been the most envied and—satirized.

Marshal De Duras, having threatened to beat Linguet to death with his stick, the latter replied :

'Marshal, you are not in the habit of using it."
This gave rise to the following lines :

> " Monsieur le Maréchal, pourquoi cette réserve,
>   Quand Linguet le prend sur ce ton ?
>   Que ne le faites-vous mourir sous le bâton
>   Afin qu'une fois il vous serve? "

> " With such forbearance, Marshal, when you treat him,
>   You lend a sting to Linguet's saucy strain.
>   France would admit, if you but turned and beat him,
>   ' *For once,*' you bore her truncheon not in vain."

History gives us several other anecdotes concerning this illustrious stick.　This one of the great Condé is familiar :

" At the battle of Fribourg in 1614, he audaciously threw his baton into the enemy's camp, and then ran to pick it up at the head of his soldiers."

And this reminds me of what an old general, a friend of mine, said to me one day: " There is one stick of command which a war chief should never hesitate to throw on the enemy's ground— it is the flag."

We must not omit this anecdote, hardly older and quite as familiar : Louis XIII. was besieging Hesdin ; having made a breach, he wanted to enter the city before the gates were opened, and cane in hand he climbed over the ramparts.　As soon as he was mounted on the breach, he turned to M. de Millerai who was following him: " make you a marshal," said he, as he presented his cane to him. " Here, take this stick ; the services that you have rendered me compel me to offer it to you."

This cane was well worth that little bit of wood, five decimètres long, covered with velvet, with eagles and lilies all over it, and crowned with a silver cap, which much more resembles a child's toy than a war emblem, and which was often bestowed through favoritism, for as these emblems multiplied, they often became rewards of actions which had nothing to do with Mars and Bellone. Madame de Sévigné says that Vivonne was made a marshal " in consideration of his future exploits."

We know that Vivonne was neither very moral nor very scrupulous, and still less warlike—but he was the brother of Madame de Montespan, the then favorite mistress of the great king—so the marshalship fell to him by right of love. On a list of names prepared by Louvois of those who were candidates for the stick, the name of Vivonne did not appear.

Madame de Montespan, who was in the habit of searching her lover's breeches pockets, found this list, and was very angry because her brother's name was not on it. She demanded that it be

8

instantly added to the list. The king himself hastened to do it " with his royal hand."

And that is how Vivonne obtained his marshal's stick.

Under Henry IV. the same cause had produced an entirely different effect. The brave Crillon, who was not rich, wanted to bear the marshal's stick in his old age, and Henry IV. would have been pleased to bestow it on him, but his mistress, Gabrielle d'Estrées, was opposed to it. Crillon, in spite of the fact that he knew she would hate him for it, had assisted Sully in preventing the king from committing the folly of marrying her.

Louis XIV., to please Madame de Montespan, gave the truncheon to Vivonne, and Henry IV., to please Gabrielle d'Estrées, refused to give it to Crillon.

A full-length portrait of Crillon is on exhibition at the Avignon Museum. The hero is represented in half court and half military dress. His left hand rests on his sword-guard, and his right on a good thick stick.

This portrait is a whole poem. The hero's martial bearing tells of his indomitable courage, his great heart, and his honesty. His sword tells of his numerous exploits, and his stick makes us pity the weakness of a king who, to please a courtesan, was unjust to the greatest captain of his age.

Henry IV. did want to give Crillon a stick, but not that of marshal of France. The king had created for his friend the place of Colonel-General of Infantry, with the right to carry the baton as a mark of that dignity.

It is said that at the seige of Charbonnières Crillon commanded the Infantry, and Sully, who had recently received the stick of the Grand Master of Artillery, stormed the place. The enemy opened a terrible fire on the two generals, who were in full view. Crillon, who was always cool, hearing the balls whiz past his ears, stopped.

"I see," said he, laughing, "that those people respect neither the stick of the Grand Master of Artillery nor that of the Colonel-General."

Henry IV., who had refused to give the truncheon to the brave Crillon, was generous in bestowing it upon his courtiers, and especially on the chiefs of the Ligue, in spite of an edict of the states of Blois held under Henry III. which said that there should only be four marshals.

In 1705 the marshals of France were particularly distinguished. Louis XIV. made them chevaliers of his orders, and added the ribbon to the stick—strange example of modesty and pride. Catinat would not accept that honor.

"I accepted the baton to fight our enemies, said he ; "I need no ribbon to do my duty."

The truncheon of the marshal of France will soon exist only in remembrance. The Revolution of 1793 broke it—the Empire re-established it ; another revolution will beak it.

This stick which from the time of Philip Augustus to our own has been borne by so many illustrious men and so many military ciphers, was dishonored in 1871 with Marshal Bazaine at Metz.

It is true that—to compensate for that—it was made illustrious in the person of Marshal MacMahon at the battle of Sedan. Seeing that the battle was lost, this brave general threw himself in the midst of the fray, crying, "I will show them how a marshal of France can die, when he can not conquer."

CHAPTER V.

THE PILGRIM'S STICK.

*The good companion.—The emblems of the pilgrim.—The pilgrims'
mass.—Blessing of the cross, the knapsack, and the stick.—The
investiture of the stick.—Pilgrims and pilgrimages of olden time.
—The legends of the pilgrims.—St. Peter's stick.—Pilgrims and
pilgrimages of to-day.*

HERE is one stick, the very thought of
which makes me smile, and which, a sym-
bol of charity, gentleness, and piety, was
always the friend and companion of man.
It is the pilgrim's stick.

It has never exercised a despotic power; it has
never been the accomplice of either the wickedness, the pride, or the vanity of the great; it
has never shed a drop of human blood nor caused
a tear to fall.

And while, during that tyrannical feudality, so
many sticks were cursed—it, the pilgrim's humble stick, was blessed by every one.

I love to go back in spirit to the middle ages,
when so many pious souls went from all points in
Christendom to visit the holy sepulchre of our
Saviour or the tomb of a saint.

8*

Their whole costume consisted of a woollen tunic and a hood. Their baggage, of a cross, a knapsack, and a stick.

But, like the chevalier who was not allowed to set out without having his weapons consecrated, the pilgrim never set out without having his cross, knapsack, and stick blessed. They were his arms!

The day of departure was a solemn one—the ceremony of blessing the emblems of his pilgrimage was also solemn. The bells rang out joyous peals; the church was decorated and illuminated as if for a feast; the pilgrim's cross, knapsack, and stick were placed upon the altar where the priest was to celebrate the mass. The pilgrim knelt in the chancel and prayed.

After mass the priest restored to him his emblems, and recited the following prayers:

BLESSING OF THE CROSS.

" Bless, Lord, this sign of the holy cross, the emblem of the journey to Jerusalem, the sign by which thou hast snatched the world from the power of the demons, and by which thou didst overcome the suggestions of the devil, who delighted in the disobedience of the first man in eating the forbidden fruit.

" Sanctify, Lord, this sign of thy passion, so that it may be a tower of strength to thy enemies, and a pledge of help for those who believe in thee."

" Brother, receive this sign and direct thy course toward the glorious sepulchre of our Redeemer, so that as thou sheddest before this sepulchre rivulets of tears, thou mayst, with divine assistance, wash away the stain of thine iniquities."

BLESSING OF THE KNAPSACK.

" In the name of our Lord Jesus Christ, receive this knapsack, the livery of thy pilgrimage, so that, being well chastened, well washed, and well cured of thy faults, thou mayst arrive at the tomb whither thou wishest to go, and that after thy journey thou mayst return to us in good health."

BLESSING OF THE STICK.

" Receive, also, this staff of thy journey in the name of our Lord Jesus Christ, who sent to his servant Tobias an angel to walk before him to serve as his guide. May it accompany thee like the angel, and guide thee whither thou wouldst go.

" May this staff be to thee a joyous companion, and may it keep far from thee all enemies; mayst thou meet no wicked men, and may the Holy Ghost deign with it to guide thy steps. By our Lord Jesus Christ, who liveth and reigneth in the unity of the Holy Ghost with God the Father, for ever and ever. Amen."

At this time the stick was not only a part of the travelling costume of the pilgrims, but it was obligatory in nearly all religious brotherhoods.

In 1241, Gregory IX. forbade the Augustins to ever go out without carrying a long stick in the form of a crutch.

It was among the monks of St. Denis that the French kings went to receive the oriflamb and the stick, when they undertook a sea voyage. It was there that Louis the young and Philip Augustus received their sticks.

Only a short time ago, monks used to travel the highways selling rosaries blessed by the pope, which they almost always bought of a dealer in the neighboring city. Some of them even pretended to come from Jerusalem, when in fact they came direct from some hermitage to which love of idleness, rather than love of prayer and meditation, had attracted them.

These pilgrims, besides the cross, the knapsack, and the stick, carried quite a respectable sized calabash, which good people always filled for them with their best wine.

The antique tradition of pilgrimages was lost, and if among these pilgrims there were simple men who took up the staff for the love of the cross, it was because there was still a spark of Christian faith in men's hearts.

I remember stories that were told me when I was yet a child. The legends of the pilgrims always excited my curiosity, and the narrator, a good old grandmother, invariably insisted upon it that " it had happened."

My grandmother had seen the stick, had touched it, and she was perhaps right, when she said " it happened," for I find the following legend of this miraculous stick in *lou grand calendrier deis bergiers, coumpousa en vers provençaou, per lou bergier de la grando mountagno,*—and the following is a nearly literal translation :

ST. PETER'S STICK.

" Voyez-vous, sur les grandes routes,
Passer le pieux pèlerin ?
Sa besace est pleine de croûtes,
Sa gourde est pleine d'un bon vin.

Son manteau gris à pèlerine
De coquillages est garni,
Et son gros chapelet béni
Se balance sur sa poitrine
A sa main est un long bâton
Que notre saint Père, dit-on,
Au bon pèlerin a fait don.

" Grâce à ce bâton, le saint homme,
Frais et dispos, suit son chemin,
Aujour d'hui revenant de Rome,
A Rome retournant demain ;
Riche malgré son indigence,
Vivant bien, mais vivant de peu ;
Ce qu'on lui donne au nom de Dieu,
Il vous le rend en indulgence.
Heureux qui touche le bâton
Qui du ciel a reçu le don
De terrasser le noir démon.

' C'est ce bâton qui lui conserve
Son teint fleuri, son pied léger ;
C'est ce bâton qui le préserve
De tout maléfice et danger.
Ce bâton, c'est l'ami fidèle,
C'est l'ange gardien qui le suit
Et qui, sans cesse, jour et nuit,
A ses côtés fait sentinelle.
Grâce soit rendue au bâton,
Dont le saint Père lui fit don
Pour être son bon compagnon.

" ' Pan ! pan ! pan ! que frappe à cette heure ?
—C'est le bâton du pèlerin.
' —Entrez, entrez dans ma demeure.
Un bon vieillard lui tend la main.

. . . .

Le soir, en faisant sa prière,
Le pèlerin disait ceci !

' Merci, mon Dieu, mon Dieu, merci !
Et gloire au bâton de Saint Pierre.
Qu'il bénisse cette maison,
Qu'il en chasse le noir démon.'
Puis il dort près de son bâton."

In our days, the rare pilgrims who still go to
Rome, to Jerusalem, or to St. Jacques de Com-
postelle, from piety do not wear the traditional
costume.   They no longer take the stick; they
take the cars.

Railroads and steamboats have robbed pilgrimages of their poetry.   It is true that we are no
longer at the epoch when Christians would have
thought they were culpably indifferent to religion,
if, taking up the emblems of the pilgrim, they had
not set out on their journey feeling very certain
of finding everywhere a generous hospitality,
which they repaid with prayers, their only treasure.

In the eleventh and twelfth centuries, these
pious peregrinations became very common.

For some time past the fashion of pilgrimages
seems to have revived in France.   We have recently seen thousands of travellers go to Notre
Dame de Lourdes and La Salette.   It was not
piety which actuated them.

Politics more than religion is now the cause of
the revival of this old practice.   Very few of

these new pilgrims, should they receive an affront, would follow the example of Robert, Duke of Normandy.

This prince had taken the staff to go and visit the tomb of Christ. A miscreant, who did not know him, cursed him, and struck him with his stick. The pious traveller only said : " A pilgrim should suffer everything for the love of God." And he kissed his cross.

This Christian resignation is not a modern virtue, and the pilgrims of to-day are no longer obliged, like those of former days, to carry the distinctive signs of pilgrimage: the cross, the knapsack, and the stick.

BOOK THIRD.

THE SUPERSTITIONS OF THE STICK.

CHAPTER I.

THE DIVINING WAND.

Mysterious powers of the stick.—What Strabon, Herodotus, Tacitus, etc., say of it.—The divining sticks of the abbeys.—How the monks used to make wood talk.—The devil's stick.—Formula for propitiating it.—The traveller's stick.—Formula for consecrating it.—Its graces and its virtues.—The charlatans of the stick.—Mesmer.—Superstition in the country and at Paris.—The secret of the divining wand.

IF the stick dates from the first tree, we may say that superstition dates from the first stick.

Circe's stick, transforming men into brutes, is the striking image of the ancient influence of the stick on the mind of feeble mortals.

History dates the divining wand back to the time when Moses and Aaron, concurrently with

9

the magicians of Egypt, performed miracles with their enchanted sticks.

Among all nations the stick has exerted a mysterious power on human beings and on the elements, and in all times impostors have used it to perpetuate prejudices, to stultify minds, and to keep alive superstition.

Strabon and Philostratus relate that the Brachmans of Persia and the Indies revealed the most secret things and predicted the future with their sticks. Herodotus speaks of the Scythians, Cicero of the Romans, Amien Marcelin of the Alains, Tacitus of the Germans, as having practiced that kind of divination.

According to Herodotus it was a stick made from a willow branch that the diviners used in the practice of their art that they had learned from their ancestors.

God upbraids his people for this superstition in Hosea :

" My people ask counsel at their stocks, and their staff declareth unto them."

Since that time wood has so often been consulted that rabdomancy is known to all the nations of the earth, and all have still a more or less lively faith in the virtues of the stick.

This superstition, fortified by the ignorance of

nations, is one of those which has done good service to charlatanry.

Divination by the stick was so generally practiced from the first ages of our history, that a council of Agde, held in 506, absolutely forbids, in its fourth canon, "any person, ecclesiastic or laie," to foretell the future. It is from this time that formulas for divination by the stick date.

The abbeys were the centre of these superstitious practices which contributed so largely to their aggrandizement, their wealth, and their domination. It was there that people went to consult the stick, which very often replied that the person consulting must give a part or even all of his wealth to the good monks. If any one refused to obey the divine prescriptions of the stick, the good monks made it speak in a much more emphatic manner.

A stick was preserved in a convent at Tolentino which the monks asserted the devil had used. This stick, in spite of its diabolical origin, had a singular virtue. It was only necessary to touch it in order to be forever safe from the torments of hell. But that touch was so high-priced, that only the rich could take advantage of this easy way of going to heaven.

This is the way the charm worked:

After having paid a stipulated sum, the penitent was allowed to place his hand on the devil's
stick in presence of the monks in prayer, one of
whom repeated in a loud voice, the following
words :

"In the name of the Father, of the Son, and
of the Holy Ghost!

"Astaroth! Astaroth! Astaroth! thou art under my dominion. Thou shalt no longer have
power over the soul of him who at this moment
holds thy stick in his hand.

"Astaroth! Astaroth! Astaroth! it is thou
who art in the power of him who holds thy stick ;
thou shalt never have dominion over him ; for he
has ransomed himself from hell through the
monks of this convent.

"In the name of the Father, and of the Son,
and of the Holy Ghost."

It is in the abbeys that the different formulas
relating to the superstitions of the stick have been
found.

A stick which has always enjoyed great consideration with our forefathers, was as remunera-
tive to the convent to which it belonged as
that of the devil was to the monks of Tolentino.

The formula which gave it the particular vir-

tues and graces with which it was endowed, was
found in an old abbey at Citeaux. It was the
monks' secret; they only revealed it for cash to
those who, before going on a journey, wanted to
have their travelling sticks consecrated.

This is the formula.

The day after All Saints' Day, break a large
branch of elder; that you must bind with iron at
the end; take out the pith, and put in its place
the eyes of a young wolf, the tongue and the
heart of a dog, three green lizards, and three
swallows' hearts between two papers sprinkled
with saltpetre; place above that, in the hollow
of the stick, seven verbena leaves, gathered on
the eve of the feast of St. John the Baptist, with
a stone of different colors, which can be found in
a lapwing's nest. Then stop up the end of the
stick with any kind of a handle you may choose,
and rest assured that this stick will protect you
from brigands, mad dogs, wild beasts, venomous
animals, and perils of all kinds; that it will know
the dangerous paths, and avoid them; and that
it will cause your entertainers to watch over you
carefully.

Now, as it was indispensable that the travelling
stick be exactly as the formula demands—which
to the poor was an impossibility—the convent al-

9*

ways kept them on hand for those who were willing to pay for them.

From the fairies of the middle ages down to the
alchemists' charlatanry, and oftener still, the love
of money have used the stick to impose upon
public credulity.　But it is from the seventeenth
and eighteenth centuries that this superstition
has become general.　Every shepherd then was
compelled to be a diviner; his wand foresaw
storms, predicted good and bad weather, and
could discover gold, silver, mercury, in the bosom
of the earth.　Even the power of discovering
thieves and assassins is imputed to them.

The story of the famous Jacques Aymard,
although familiar, deserves to be related here.

A man and his wife were assassinated in 1692,
at Lyons, in a cellar.　One Jacques Aymard, who
made a business of tracking thieves and murderers, was sent for.　He was taken before the king's
prosecutor, to whom he made a promise to track
the guilty parties, and to overtake them, provided
he would be allowed to begin at the place where
the murder was committed.　He descended into
the cellar, having in his hand a wand.　He became agitated, his pulse beat rapidly in the two
places where the corpses of the man and woman
had been found.　Guided by his stick, Aymard

THE DIVINING STICK.

followed the steets through which the assassins had passed, walked along the Rhone, escorted by three persons stopped everywhere where the thieves had stopped, and, in short, tracked them to Beaucaire, where he caught one of the murderers, a little hunchback, who confessed his crime, and was executed at Lyons.

But this was not enough. He had accomplices. Aymard again took up his stick and set out, passed through Nîmes, came back to Toulon, where he discovered that the thieves had sailed; he sailed also, and found them in the little village of Seyne.

The author of the story of this famous diviner, a physician, relates other phenomena due to the stick of his hero, and seeing nothing unnatural in it, by the rules of emotion established by Descartes, and by the existence of *subtile matter*, insists upon it that we are " only astonished at this power of the stick, because we are not so familiar with it as with that of the loadstone." No one so simple as a learned man.

Neither Dr. Carner's book nor the book that Boyle had already written on the same subject could prevent public credulity from attributing to supernatural causes the phenomena of the divining wand.

So when Mesmer arrived in Paris with his enchanted stick in his hand, it was easy for him to
make numerous adepts, and to assemble around his
mysterious tub crowds of all classes of society,
whose enthusiasm was boundless.   When Mesmer
was declared a prophet, his wand was accepted as
a principle, and his hocus-pocus set up as a doctrine.

When will human beings become convinced that
the most marvellous phenomena have only a purely
natural cause?

Even in Paris, there are numerous believers in
these superstitious practices.   Men in communi-
cation with spirits, find simpletons willing to pay
very dear for their magic herbs, moss boiled with
toads, mandsagora, and azedarach, over which they
have pronounced the grand cabalistic formula of
Solomon.

We must not be astonished if in many villages,
in the south of France especially, diviners are
consulted, who for money will predict the future
or discover hidden objects by turning the
stick.

In order to make the charm successful, it is
indispensably necessary for the stick to possess
all the conditions required by magic, and the following formula must be scrupulously employed:

SECRET OF THE DIVINING WAND.

As soon as the sun rises in the horizon, take in your hand a virgin branch of the wild hazel-nut tree ; strip off its leaves, and say : " I pick thee up in the name of Elohim, Mutrothon, and Semiphoras, so that you may possess the virtue of the wands of Moses and Aaron, to discover all that I may want to know."

To make it work, say :

" I command thee in the name of Elohim, Mutrothon, Adonai, and Semiphoras."

Let us hope that, thanks to the light of reason, and to instruction which is being diffused through the country, the divining wand will soon exist only in our gardens, under the peaceful form of a flower --Jacob's stick.

CHAPTER II.

THE AUGURAL STICK.

The augury priests among the Romans.—Divination with closed doors.—How the augury worked.—The priest auguring among the Germans.—Their manner of operating.—Origin of the augural stick.

 STICK which formerly had an extraordinary influence over the minds of the people, and to which superstition ascribed supernatural virtues, was the litnus pontificus of the Roman augurs, called the augural stick.

The powers of this stick were very great: it could decide for peace or war; its oracles immediately became articles of faith ; its was consulted before every serious affair.

Cicero said that two augurs could not look at each other without laughing. The great orator must have known whereof he spoke, for he himself had been an oracle. But the people did not laugh at them. They accepted the predictions of the oracles as judgments from heaven, and woe to the one who tried to undeceive them. There were no freethinkers at Rome then.

And yet educated people no more believed in the divine virtue of the augural stick, than they believe to-day in the miracles of La Salette; but as it was to their advantage to let the people wallow in ignorance, and compulsory education, that peaceful weapon, which is destined to convulse the old world, was not yet invented, it was easy for the educated to prevent their fellow-citizens from discovering the arts of divination. In order to keep the secrets of religion from the public, the oracle was never divested of his augural stick, and was always elected by the oracles themselves.

The augural stick was first, at Rome, a political means for arbitrary action. The first kings used it as the first instrument of domination. It then became, in the hands of the priests, the easiest way of keeping alive superstition. The oracle was consulted not only on public, but on private affairs.

This is the manner in which the priests were supposed to operate—for the public was not admitted to this ceremony—that we may call divination with closed doors; it is very certain that the celebration of the augural mystery only existed in the imagination of believers.

The pontiff held in his hand his litnus, a long stick, but in the form of a crosier. He is dressed in his *toga auguralis*, a long, red dress. He turns gravely to the east, and points with his stick to a certain part of the sky. This part of the sky is called *templum*. The pontiff looks to see what birds appear, and on what part of the templum they fly.

If they fly to the right, it is a lucky sign; if to the left, it is unlucky.

The people never doubted that the pontiff had performed his office conscientiously and in the prescribed form, when he rendered his oracle.

There was also a public consultation of the oracle. This was a solemn proceeding, and more impressive than the other.

On a stormy day, when Jupiter thundered in the clouds, the pontiff, dressed in a long scarlet robe, with a pointed hat on his head and his augural stick in his hand, climbed to the very top of a mountain, whence he could see all parts of the horizon. Crowds of people followed him religiously. Having arrived at the very summit, he offered a sacrifice to the gods, addressed a prayer to them, in which the spectators joined, then turning towards the east, showed with his stick the point of the heavens which he wished

to observe ; then if lightning gleamed and thunder roared, the oracle had answered ; perhaps
favorably, perhaps unfavorably, according to the
direction from which the thunder and lightning
came. Hope and fear filled all hearts. It would
seem that the elements obeyed the diviner's
stick, and that Jupiter himself inspired him.

The augurs used other means of divination in
which the stick was less conspicuous, but in which
the imposition was as great. One of the commonest of them was the oracle rendered according
to chickens' appetites.

If they eagerly devoured the food offered to
them by the pontiff, the presage was favorable ;
it was fatal if they refused to eat it. The priests
could easily obtain whatever oracles they wished
for ; the chickens were confided to their care, and
they had only to starve them more or less.

According to Tacitus, the Germans also had much
faith in oracles. "Their manner of consulting
them," said he, " is very simple : several twigs are
cut from a fruit-tree ; after having distinguished
them by some mark, they are thrown pell-mell
into some white material ; then the city priest, if
it is about public affairs, or the father of a family,
if it is about private interests, having offered a
prayer to the gods, and looking towards heaven,

10

raises each stick three times one after the other, and interprets them according to the different order in which the different marks are presented.

The origin of the augural stick dates back to Romulus, who was, we know, well versed in the art of divination. It is to this king that the institution of oracles is due, and it is his stick which served for a model for the litnus pontificus.

This stick of Romulus is a whole legend.

When Camillus re-entered Rome, plundered and devastated by the barbarians, he immediately sought out the sites of all the sacred places. Having arrived at the chapel of Mais, after having made the tour of the palatinum, which was a pile of ashes, those who were searching discovered Romulus's stick uninjured. While everything around had been consumed by the fire, only the pontifical stick of the royal diviner had remained whole and uninjured.

"The Romans were extremely elated at this discovery," says Plutarch, "and it made them very hopeful for Rome; they had no doubt that the sign presaged for it an eternal duration."

The priests preserved religiously the stick of Romulus among other sacred things. Its miraculous preservation had made it an object of veneration.

To-day the litnus pontificus is replaced by the crosier, but bishops do not predict the future with it ; they now have a much more potent arm with which to govern the people, and that is knowledge, and those of them who command our respect, command it, not by their crosiers, but by their virtues.

The Druid religion, which originated in the forests, and whose worship consisted in the veneration of the oak, used the stick as a means of moral domination.

Like Oginius, the Gallic orator, who harangued the people stick in hand, the Druids gave their oracles with a white or magic wand in their hands.

For centuries the enchanted stick of the Druids was among the Gauls the accomplice of superstition, and presided at bloody ceremonies in mysterious groves.

The Druidesses, who styled themselves fairies, and who shared the priesthood with the Druids, also foretold the future, wand in hand.

According to an old tradition of the inhabitants of the mountains in the department of Aude, in the ancient country of Kereorb, the priestesses, called the *Encantados* (the enchanted), used a wand of gold to knock the fruit off trees. This

wand even had the power of carrying them anywhere into space.   When they wanted to traverse
a valley or cross a ravine, they had only to lean
on their magic wand, which, lengthening itself
indefinitely, served for a support.   .

The stick no longer performs such wonders, but
it is still used in the country to knock the fruit
from trees.   The golden wand of the Druidesses
has become the long pole used to gather nuts,
almonds, and olives.

CHAPTER III.

SUPERNATURAL STICKS.

*Mahomet's Stick.—Its wonders.—What happened when they tried
to take it out of the Mosque of Medina.—Story of the Sticks of
Haroun Al Raschid, of a giant, and a dwarf.—Story of Bahalul,
the fool.—A Turkish proverb.*

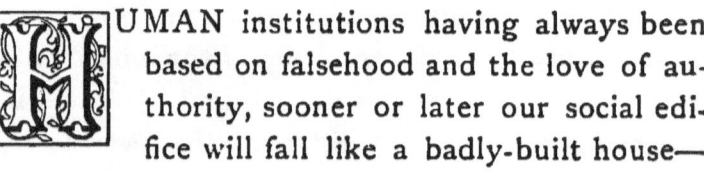UMAN institutions having always been
based on falsehood and the love of au-
thority, sooner or later our social edifice will fall like a badly-built house—
it was an impossibility that the stick, the sign of
authority par excellence, should not become a

universal agent of superstition, that eternal sister of falsehood.

Among the Mahometans where, happier than a constitutional king, the stick reigns and governs by the side of the constitutional cimetar, Mahomet, a pontiff king like Romulus, wanted, like him, to have his stick worshipped.

This indefatigable stick, which had so often accompanied the prophet from Medina to Mecca, before which so many people had prostrated themselves, and which, among its other miracles, had cut the moon in two; this terrible stick, which for the conquering legislator was the best argument of persuasion wherever he wished to establish his doctrine, and with which he had broken one by one the three hundred and sixty idols in the caaba of Mecca, deserved, more than any other, to be classed with sacred things.

On the day of Mahomet's death, or rather his ascension into heaven, his stick was placed in a mosque of Medina; there it was religiously preserved, and pilgrims never set out for Mecca without addressing a prayer to it.

In 673, the Caliph Moaviab, understanding how advantageous this stick might be to Ali's proselytes, who at that time inhabited the ancient

10*

capital of Arabia, tried to take possession of it in order to carry it to Damas.

By his order, his soldiers arrived at Medina, entered the mosque where the remains of the apostle were, but as they were about to touch the stick with their sacrilegious hands, the sun was obscured, and darkness enshrouded the city ; the inhabitants were in the greatest consternation, and the soldiers drew back in alarm without daring to touch the sacred instrument. Upon hearing of this phenomenon, Moaviab abandoned his project.

The city of Damas, however, did not cease to covet the prophet's stick, and in 703 Abdel Malec, who had just been proclaimed caliph, also tried to obtain possession of it to place it in a mosque of the Holy City, which was the seat of government.

For this purpose he made the journey to Medina, unwilling that any one but himself should undertake this important mission. As he was about to lay his hand on the stick an inhabitant of Medina cried out, " Commander of the Faithful, give up this project. Moaviab attempted it before you. This sacrilege would bring misfortune upon you—and the prophet would curse you."

These words stopped the arm of Abdel Malec,

who, like Moaviab, did not dare to brave superstition by touching Mahomet's stick.

Another legendary stick among the Turks is that of Haroun Al Raschid. This monarch was in the habit of roaming about nights in the streets of his good city of Bagdad, with an enormous stick in his hand, and always accompanied by his favorite slave, Mesrour.

One night, as they were returning to his palace, they suddenly found themselves in the presence of two men who were disputing. One of them, a perfect Hercules, carried a large stick; the other, an undersized man, had no weapon; he looked like a dwarf beside the giant. Haroun Al Raschid and Mesrour stopped, and naturally began to protect the smaller.

"Vile miscreant," said the tall one, as he brandished his stick, "if I did not pity thee, I would kill thee like a dog as thou art, for the miserable turban thou didst sell so dear; give me back my gold."

"Give me back the turban, and I will give you back part of your money, but not all, for my work is worth something."

"By Allah!" exclaimed the angry giant, "thy work deserves blows; defend thyself if thou canst, or flee from my wrath, accursed slave."

At these words Haroun Al Raschid approached the little man and said, as he handed him his stick, " Here, defend thyself."

The little man mechanically took the stick, but he had hardly touched this formidable weapon when the giant uttered a cry of terror and fled in dismay. At this sight the dwarf, overwhelmed with astonishment, prostrated himself at the feet of his liberator and returned him his stick.

" What is this enchanted weapon which has put to flight the strongest of men," said he, in a voice trembling with emotion.

Haroun eluded the question. "What is that man's name," said he, "and why was he going to strike you ? "

" That man," replied the dwarf, "is Abdoul Amoun, one of the richest merchants of the city ; he is very strong ; he might have killed me with a blow from his hand. I am called Firouz, the Persian, and I am a tailor. I was going home when Abdoul Amoun met me, and quarrelled with me about a turban which I sold him ; but surely he must have been intoxicated, or he never would have quarrelled with a poor slave like me."

" Then how do you account for his flight ? "

" By the will of God, who always protects the weak man, especially when he has not violated the laws of the prophet, for my turban was worth the gold that Abdoul gave me," added the tailor, who wanted to pass for a conscientious merchant.

On entering his palace, Haroun Al Raschid sent for Giafar, his prime minister, and having related his adventure of the night, ordered him to send for Abdoul Amoun the merchant, and Firouz the Persian tailor, and to question them in his presence.

A few minutes after the giant and the dwarf, more dead than alive, appeared before the caliph and prostrated themselves at the foot of the throne. Each had thoroughly examined his conscience, but could find nothing in either his actions or his words which resembled a crime against the state; but for all that they trembled. The caliph, the vizier, the judges, the bastinado, perhaps death, terrified them.

"Abdoul Amoun," cried Giafar, in his gravest voice, "thou knowest that nothing which occurs at Bagdad, day or night, is unknown to us. Thou art here before the commander of the believers, and of justice, which punishes falsehood; answer then truthfully. Tell us why thou, a giant, wouldst have struck and probably killed this poor dwarf?"

"I swear before the commander of the believers to tell the truth," said the poor merchant. "I ac-

cuse myself, and I repent. I don't know what evil
genius urged me on—I beg pardon."

"Mind your answers Abdoul Amoun," said the
grand vizier sententiously, who could hardly re-
frain from laughing at the pitiful mien of the
accused. "You are not telling the truth—you
do know what evil genius urged you to do evil;
you had drunk wine; you were intoxicated,"
added Giafar in an angry tone.

At this terrible accusation, poor guilty Abdoul
Amoun thought he was lost. His only answer
was to strike the floor with his forehead three
times. It was a confession of guilt, and an act
of contrition at the same time.

"Abdoul Amoun," continued the vizier, "you
must now tell us why you fled as soon as Firouz
took up the stick to defend himself, after you had
provoked him to it."

"Why, why," muttered the poor merchant, as
he raised his pale and dusty face, "it was because
I thought I saw in his hand the prophet's stick."

Haroun Al Raschid had a very wise fool. His
name was Bahalul. One day the monarch ordered him to make a list of all the fools in Bagdad. "Lord," replied Bahalul, "it would take
too long. If you want the list of sane people, I
can give it to you in an instant."

Another time he entered the audience chamber of the celebrated caliph, and finding the throne vacant, he placed himself upon it and played the judge. The guards chased him off, and belabored him about the shoulders. He was weeping when Haroun Al Raschid entered the room.

" Why dost thou weep, Bahalul ? "

" Alas, Lord, it is not because I have been beaten, but out of pity for you, for I have de-served the stick for sitting on the throne a single moment ; what must you expect, who sit on it every day ? "

The next day he was found dead, and the people believed that Heaven had punished him for having sat on the caliph's throne, and touched his stick.

There were strange prejudices concerning Haroun Al Raschid's stick. Some said it had belonged to Mahomet, and that if this illustrious caliph had once been able to·make the journey to Mecca on foot, the credit belonged to his stick. Others insisted that this stick was that of the celebrated Omar, of which Alvakedi, the Arabian historian said : " Omar's stick inspired more dread than the swords of his successors."

And thus in order to justify to themselves their weakness and cowardice, people willingly accord supernatural powers to the arm which rules them and the stick which strikes them. Fear is one of the surest agents of superstition, and that is why, from the very beginning of human society, people have prostrated themselves before despots.

A Turkish proverb says: " If you would be adored, be feared. If you would be feared, be a despot. If you would be a despot, be a stick and strike."

CHAPTER IV.

PROLIFIC STICKS.

The Stick of the temple of Juno at Athens.—The love of maternity.—The right of women to bachelors.—Marriages by the grace of blows from a Stick.—Male Sticks and female Sticks.

 KNOW of nothing in the world, to which so many mysterious powers have been attributed as to the stick. In Greece, emperors generally used it to cure all sorts of diseases. Certain sticks possessed by priests, even had the power to make women fruitful.

TEMPLE OF JUNO.

In Athens, when a woman after one year of marriage had not had a child, she went to the temple of Juno, where a stick was kept to which the goddess who presides over births had given the power of fecundation. A lupercal priest performed the ceremony in this manner :

The sterile woman went to the temple of Juno, took off her clothes, lay down on the floor, and the priest gave her nine well-directed blows with a stick. Nine months after, the republic had a new inhabitant.

In the parochial church at Apt, a department of Vancluse, the little cradle, which, according to popular belief, is that of Saint Anne, is religiously preserved. This cradle, in which the mother of the Virgin Mary slept in her infancy, also has the gift of fecundation. Sterile women have only to rock it nine months, and nine months after they are sure of a child.

If at Athens births were sometimes due to the mysterious stick preserved in the temple of Juno, marriages were made by a means almost as singular.

With this people, who cared for nothing so much as for the aggrandizement of the republic, celibacy was looked upon with aversion. When a bachelor passed by in the street, women had a right—which they used—to run after him, and

11

beat him with a stick; so either through patriotism or fear of the bastinado, all bachelors married
sooner or later.

According to travellers in certain provinces of
China, prolific sticks are highly venerated; and are
very profitable to the *bonzes*, or priests, who keep
them. These impostors pretend that in certain
sticks preserved in their pagodas, spirits live who
preside over births. The priests call good births
the birth of a boy, and bad births the birth of a
girl.

When a woman wants the prolific influence of
the stick she goes to the bonze, who for money,
or if she is pretty, for nothing, hastens to officiate
for her.

This is the way the ceremony is performed:

The woman goes to the pagoda dressed in her
finest clothes; the bonze gravely takes her by
the hand, and conducts her majestically to the
foot of the altar, where incense is burning. As
soon as they reach the altar steps, musicians
make the church walls resound with their shrill,
discordant instruments.

In the middle of the altar stands a massive
statue with large bosoms, and great round eyes;
at the foot of the altar lies a long box full of
sticks—male and female sticks. On each stick

unintelligible characters are written. While the bonze mutters prayers no less unintelligible than the sentences, the woman casually pulls a stick out of the box, and hands it to the officiating priest, who explains the meaning of the sentence written on the stick. The oracle nearly always promises a happy delivery, and that is why women so often consult it.

When the prediction is not verified, no blame is attached to the bonze; some evil genius, which was in the woman's womb when he was rendering his oracle, had destroyed the charm of his sticks.

These marvellous sticks are really not without influence on sterility—but the ceremonies required of them are only performed with closed doors.

Thus priests of all religions have the power to accomplish—in a mysterious manner—many things apparently supernatural, which we must be permitted to think are often quite natural.

CHAPTER V.

THE STICK AMONG THE SAVAGES.

Credulity of the Savages.—They pray to the Stick which rules them.—The Stick of the tree which grows only in Heaven.—The Stick of the Indian chiefs.—The Arikis.—The Makontou.—The Stick of the savages of the extreme north of America.—The Chitombe.—Celestial origin of his royal Stick.—The grand Pontiff.—The Gnombo.—How they prevent a king from dying.—How to become a Chitombe.—Strange manner of electing a king recommended to civilized nations.—Consecration by the Stick.

SAVAGE chiefs, like civilized kings, gen erally carry a stick of command. The only difference is, that the savages never making war by proxy—as our monarchs do—this symbol of their dignity is nothing less than emblematic, and that the most revered of sticks is that which has slain the greatest number of enemies; just as it used to be in heroic times.

Savages are generally weak-minded; ignorance makes them crudulous; so the grossest superstitions, the most stultifying prejudices are to them beliefs which no amount of reasoning can ever destroy. In this they are like the ignorant classes in civilized countries.

It is to the interests of the chiefs to keep alive these superstitions; without them they could not govern. They allow them to believe that their stick is made of the branch of a tree that grows only in heaven, or that God himself has given it to them. It is quite common to see savages entreating the stick of their chief not to harm them, or to cure them of a disease, or to preserve them from the evil spirit, whether the stick to which they parley belong to a king, a priest, or a magician, for with barbarians, as with civilized nations, those are the powers which have united to perpetuate ignorance, to keep alive superstition, and seizing by despotism—of which the *stick*, sceptre or wand, sabre or sword, is the truest, the best representation.

Baugainville, in his journey around the world, saw the Indian chiefs who were under the dominion of the Dutch company have sticks. These sticks were generally four or five feet long, and painted red.

In New Zealand the religious chiefs, Arikis, carry one like a crosier, which is supposed to be *Makoutou*, that is enchanted. The Makoutou is a ontinual source of fear to those poor Islanders. They attribute diseases to it, and believe it has the power to prevent them from dying. The Arikis

11*

has only to utter a few words and to make certain gestures or grimaces in order to perform his enchantments for good or evil, according to the will of the chief.

"Your Makoutou is absurd," said a. missionary, to a savage; "I have braved it a thousand times, and no misfortune has happened to me."

" Because," replied the Islander, " you too are an Arikis; you have as powerful a God who protects you, as the gods of this country."

" But I have told you that my God is yours also, and that the gods that your Arikis preach do not exist."

" My Arikis is wiser than you, and he says they do, and I know very well that if I did not believe him the gods of my country would turn their anger against me and mine."

Wherever we look, in the still numerous uncivilized countries, we find a more or less feudal government, where a multitude of petty tyrants exercise an absolute power, and each chief manufactures a stick to suit himself, according as he wishes to strike the imagination or the backs of his subjects.

" And that proves," says a traveler, " that the despotic governments are those which approach the nearest to those of barbarians."

In the extreme north of America the civil chiefs carry a stick whose only ornament is the bone of a cariboo. The jugglers or musicians, or medicine-men, who have absolute control over the chiefs even, make the most of the fear of death and the ambition of a good chase, to impose upon them by all sorts of juggleries and divinations with a stick rubbed with an herb whose virtues they alone know.

Among the savages of Louisiana, when a warrior dies, his successor pronounces his funeral oration, holding in his hand the stick of the dead chief. As soon as he has ceased speaking, the assistants present themselves naked before him, and he gives to each three heavy blows, saying: "Remember, that in order to be a good warrior like the deceased, you must know how to suffer."

The Congo negroes have for a civil and religious chief a grand pontiff, called the Chitombe. His symbol is an enormous stick, which he only carries on great occasions. When the negroes go to war they are allowed to touch it, and become invincible from the moment they do so.

This stick is hereditary; its origin is celestial; it was given by God himself at the beginning of the world to the first Chitombe; it is the symbol of dynastic government, and of divine right.

"Take this stick, and be the grand pontiff,'
said God to the first of the Chitombes.

"And what can I do with that stick?" replied
the first of the Chitombes.

"When thou art sick or in danger of death,
give it to Gnombo, who will be thy great prophet."

"And what will the great prophet do with it?"

"He will immediately kill thee, *to prevent thee
from dying*, and will become grand pontiff in thy
place."

These people believe, that if their Chitombe
died a natural death, the heavens and the earth
would be destroyed, so in order to avoid this
calamity, and in obedience to God's order, as
soon as they consider the grand pontiff in danger
of death, the grand prophet kills him with the
hereditary stick intended for that purpose, and
becomes the Chitombe. The new Chitombe immediately nominates a Gnombo, whose duty it
it will be to kill him, and so on.

If this right of inheriting should become general,
sceptres would be less envied.

Another no less queer way of electing kings would
likewise tend to cool off aspirants to royalty if it
became general, and this one is practiced among
certain tribes of India. The whole nation must
be of opinion that the candidate for the sover-

eign power has given proof of valor in war, that
he is skillful in handling the stick, and in drawing the bow, and that he knows how to suffer
pain ; and in order to make sure of this last condition, he is conducted into the plain, where each
Indian of any note gives him as many blows with
the stick as he can, and the recipient of these
striking attentions must not even utter a sigh. If
a single complaint escapes him, he is declared un-
worthy to ever become the chief of the nation.

That might be called consecration by the stick.

It is well known that the Japanese are naturally
superstitious, but what is less known, is their great
devotion to the god Kaca. This divinity has his
temple on the top of a very high mountain, to
which the pious go every year on a pilgrimage,
accompanied by the bonzes, who call themselves
his disciples. These disciples of Kaca carry
heavy sticks to castigate the pilgrims. The more
blows the latter receive *en route*, the more favorable will their god be to them. Those who die
under the bastinado go straight to heaven.

That might be called sanctification by the stick.

In this, the disciples of the god Kaca are not
more superstitious than we ourselves were formerly, alas! and than we are to-day, even. In
another part of this history we will see all over

Catholic Europe the same superstition inspiring the same fanaticism. We will see clerical fustigation given and accepted, not only as a means of salvation, but even become obligatory in certain practices of religion.

Thus among civilized people as among savages, religious and political chiefs used the stick to keep alive among the people the fanaticism which makes slaves, and the superstition which creates fanaticism.

The world, being governed by material as well as by moral force, man seems to be fatally condemned to submit to the yoke of despotic authority, of which the stick is the striking image. But as to-day, thanks to philosophy, man, before kneeling to force, asks himself if nature has given one man the right to govern all, and good sense answers No, it follows that people no longer submit willingly to despotic authority, and that they are always ready to throw off the yoke forcibly put upon them.

BOOK FOURTH.

USES AND CUSTOMS OF THE STICK.

CHAPTER I.

The Stick the sceptre of the legitimate kings of the fireside.—The old men of Argos.—Majesty of the Stick.—The Stick among the Athenians.—The Stick among the Israelites.—Tamar and Judah. —Betrothal by the Stick.—The Stick among the Romans.—The Lictors.—Fecial Priests.—War and peace, servitude and liberty— by the Stick.

ROM a picturesque point of view, and in its purely technical meaning, the stick, properly so-called, is a narrow piece of wood, inflexible, about a yard long, and which serves as a support in walking.

Well, this simple piece of wood, to which we attach no importance except for the services that it renders us, and which we often carelessly throw into a corner, this stick, however plain it may be, obtrudes itself more than any other object upon the meditations of the philosopher and the thinker. We have seen it under different forms and names, on the throne and on the altar, in public and in private life. We shall see it again, under different forms and names, exert its sovereign influence in all classes of society.

Formerly the stick was not only a sign of distinction among the humblest individuals, but with some nations the carrying of it was obligatory. Among the Babylonians, for instance, no man could go out without a stick. It was the distinctive mark of the principal dignitaries. Fathers of families carried them of a peculiar form and with peculiar emblems, in accordance with their position. It was the sceptre of these legitimate kings of the fireside. No one was allowed to go out without a simple and naked stick—each one had to bear a distinctive mark.

With nearly all the people of Arabia, the stick, no less obligatory, represented not only the family, but the tribe ; and even to-day, most of the families or nomadic tribes, who travel over Europe, and whom we call Bohemians, carry a long, knobbed stick.

The Greeks carried a stick bent in the form of a crosier. M. Leconte de l'Isle, in his *Evynnies* speaks of the old men of Argos, leaning on their bent sticks, and deploring the fate of the illustrious chiefs and soldiers who fell under the walls of Ilion. This stick—the most majestic of all sticks —added to the natural gravity of the old men.

At Athens, when a long journey was contemplated, all the members of the family were called together, and all the friends, and libations were poured to the traveller's stick.

The pouring of libations was the Pagan way of worshipping God.

Sometimes the stick was given as a letter of recommendation. In that case the seal of the one who gave it was inlaid upon the stick. To lend one's stick was the greatest proof of esteem and friendship that could be given.

Among the Israelites the stick often served as a pledge to a promise.

" What wilt thou give me," said Tamar to Judah, "that thou mayst come in unto me?"

" I will send thee a kid from my flock," replied Judah.

But Tamar, doubtless having no very great faith in this promise, wanted a pledge before granting favors.

And she said, " Wilt give me a pledge till thou send it?"

12

And he said, " What pledge shall I give thee ? "

And she said, " Thy signet, and thy bracelets, and thy staff that is in thine hand."

For the rest of the adventure see 38th chapter of Genesis.

The stick also served as a promise of marriage. In that case it was cut in two, and the young man and the young woman each took a half, which they preserved carefully until the wedding day. On that day they presented to the priest the two halves of the stick, which, joined together by him, were the symbol of the promised union.

This was betrothal by the stick.

In Rome, where the stick was conspicuous in all religious ceremonies, where it presided at the most important political acts, it was a representation of justice, as well as an emblem of certain civil and military offices. There was even the judgment of the *pike* rendered by the Centumvirs *hastam cogere.*

In the hands of the lictors, as in those of the centurions, it represented not only justice but also chastisement.

The business of the lictors was to precede consuls and senators. When these magistrates went out, woe to those who forgot to kneel as they passed, or who did not open their houses quickly enough when they wanted to enter, for the lictors stood by with raised stick.

The police of the streets and of the forum was under their charge. The people feared and hated them, for they were at the same time bailiffs and executioners; and the emblem of their office was too willingly an instrument of oppression. The noblest of their functions is to walk before the triumphal cars. We may say that the sticks of the lictors were the representation of tyranny, royal as well as republican.

The stick in the hands of the heralds-at-arms declared war, and also proclaimed peace.

The most contrary things were symbolized by the stick. To-day an instrument of servitude, to-morrow it became a sign of liberty. A blow with a stick to a slave was the sign of his freedom, and it was by the stick that he was kept under the yoke.

The stick was not even a stranger to marriage. When a girl married it was customary to part her hair in two with the point of a pike, and to offer her a stick. According to Plutarch, this pike represented the javelins which the Romans used at the rape of the Sabine women. According to other authors. it related to Juno, to whom the lance was consecrated. The most accredited opinion is, that the *stick*, lance, pike, or javelin, was a symbol of courage. A pike was placed on the head of the bride to signify that she would give birth to courageous men, and a stick was given her to signify that she would, be her husband's staff, and would follow him everywhere, even into dangers.

The Romans and the Chinese have accorded the most power, and surrounded with the greatest prestige, this slender piece of wood which might be called the great justiciary of nations, and which, from the earliest times, under all sorts of names and shapes, has played such a variety of parts on the world's great stage.

CHAPTER II.

THE STICK AMONG THE MODERNS.

Signature by the Stick.—The Stick an emblem of property.—Garnishment by the Stick.—Divorce.—Why Louis VII. could not enter the church of Notre Dame, and what he gave as a pledge to the canons of Creteil.—Inheritance by the Stick.—My father's Stick.—Moral.

S we have copied much from the Romans, the stick has necessarily played a conspicuous part with us, and we see it figure to great advantage in our old customs. The fear of it which the feudal lords inspired, awakened in the minds of the people, together with the idea of punishment consequent upon the inobservance of the laws, respect for every act which it was used to sanction.

As we have seen in another part of this history, there was no appeal from the laws of the stick, and no disowning the contracts or agreements in which it had been accepted as a witness—the stick was often used as a witness to an agreement, and for this purpose it sufficed that each party to the agreement make some mark with a knife upon the stick of the other.

12*

At this time, when writing was almost unknown except in monasteries, this kind of signature was much used.

With us, also, the stick was long a sign of possession and property. When land, or any other property, was transferred to another, the transferrer placed his stick in the hands of the transferree, and the sale was made.* That usage, or one similar to it, is still practiced in many of the provinces for the sale of cattle at fairs. When the sale is concluded, the purchaser returns to the seller his stick.

The stick placed upon property, prevented its sale; but all proprietors were not liable to find their possessions thus mortgaged. There were some upon whose property neither guard, nor pledge, nor lordly stick could be placed.—These were the nobles.

While the stick was used to take possession of property, it was also used in its relinquishment before a feudal lord. That sort of contract was called *main au bâton.*

If among the ancients betrothals were made by the stick, in France, under the first and second

---

* We have already seen, that when the Frankish chiefs were invested with the sovereign power, a stick with two bent crockets was placed in their hands. This stick then became their sceptre.

races, it was by the stick that divorces were obtained. The parties had only to present themselves before the judge in public audience, and,
without trial, break, one after the other, sticks of
alder, and throw the pieces at the foot of the tribunal. The husband, in thus breaking the symbol of his matrimonial power, gave back to his
wife her former freedom. This was divorce by
the stick.

The stick was also given and received as a
pledge of honor. History furnishes many instances of this, the following among others:

Louis the VII., giddy, but very devout, was in
the habit of going every day, in all sorts of
weather, to hear mass at Notre Dame. One day
he found the door closed.

" Holloa ! " cried the king through the keyhole,
" is there no one here to-day ? "

" I am here—the beadle," replied a voice in the
church.

" Why is the door closed ? "

" Sire, it is by order of the canonical lords."

" But why have the canonical lords given that
order ? "

A voice which was not that of the beadle, replied :

" Sire, contrary to all the customs and liberties

of Notre Dame, you supped last night at Creteil,
not at your own expense, but at that of the body
corporate of this holy church ; that is why mass
is not celebrated to-day, and the door is closed ;
the canons have resolved to bear any suffering
rather than to allow any infringement of their
rights.'

"I did not offend with premeditated design,"
answered Louis, still through the keyhole. "The
inhabitants of Creteil entertained me without
force or compulsion. I am sorry," added the
poor king, in a contrite tone ; "send for Bishop
Thibaud, Dean Clement, the canons, and the pro-
vost of Creteil. If I have done wrong, I wish to
atone for it."

The king remained in prayer before the door
of the church while awaiting the arrival of these
dignitaries. When they appeared he made his
apology, the door was opened, and the services
began. After mass the affair was investigated,
and Louis was condemned to pay an indemnity,
inasmuch as he had not the right of hospitality
at the house of the canons of Creteil, and they
being the owners of the inhabitants, his accepting
the supper of these poor people was an outrage
on them, and a very serious offense against the
church.

The monarch acknowledged that the penalty was just, and as he had no money with him, he gave as a pledge the person of the bishop himself. That security would not, perhaps, have quite satisfied the canons, if Louis had not, to prove still further by an outward act that he was really desirious of repaying to the chapter the expense to which he had put the people of Creteil, placed upon the altar the stick which he held in his hand.

There are certain customs of the stick whose meaning it is difficult to understand ; this one for instance : When, in order to free himself from a debt or a fine which he could not pay, a debtor wished to compel his nearest relative to pay it for him, he had but to throw a handful of dirt at him, and jump over a hedge, holding a stick in his hand.

In those good old times, as people say now—no doubt by antiphrasis—the nobles had a way of paying their creditors which it is much easier to understand ;. they paid them with blows with a stick, which they called *chasse-coquins.* There are many nobles to-day who would willingly pay their debts in the same manner, but we no longer live in those good old times.

If, as we have already seen, the investiture of royal and episcopal authority was made by the sceptre and the crosier, the king conferred fiefs and benefices by the ring and the stick. The ring signified fidelity and constancy, and the stick was symbolic of the authority of the lord, and the subjection of the vassal.

This double representation of the stick is what gives it its originality. It was bestowed upon the nobles as a mark of nobility and command, and upon the people as a sign of plebeiance and obedience.

When a novice was received in the orders of chivalry, he was given a light blow with a stick— it was his baptism. Once a chevalier he could no longer use this weapon in the jousts of the tournament, nor on those who forgot to uncover their heads as he passed.

The stick was long carried by court people of both sword and gown as an offensive weapon, and the common people had no great reason to be overjoyed at this, for it was on their humble backs that the blows fell.

The use, or rather the abuse, of the stick became so great that Charlemagne ordered " that no one, no matter what his rank, should carry such an arm or stick; his officers must abandon them immediately, under penalty of being chastised as an example."

Of all the ordinances which redound to the glory of Charlemagne, this is not the least wise. Monarchs so rarely make laws for the benefit of the common people, that when by chance we meet with one who does, we ought to be glad to record the fact.

The stick was also an heir-loom. The father bequeathed it to the most deserving member of his family. It was a great honor to inherit a father's stick. I understand and admire that custom.

Who can look without emotion on his old father's stick? It is himself I see, under the tall trees surrounding my abode, his noble head crowned with silver hair; I hear his voice calling to me for the support of my arm, me, his other staff of old age, and I hasten to him, happy in the thought that I, too, can be a support to him. While the old man's left hand rested on my shoulder, his right hand rested on you, oh stick! you remind me of those blessed hours of promenade, during which, like the ancient peripatetic, my old father gave me lessons of wisdom which have always been the guide of my life. Yes, this stick is indeed himself. "Remember," said he, " that I have ever walked in the narrow way, and that it is only in thus following in my footsteps that you can honor my memory."

CHAPTER III.

JOURNEYINGS WITH THE STICK.

Journeying on foot, Stick in hand.—Janus, Ceres, and Triptolème
—What happened to a king who asked Bacchus for much gold.—
Cato's repentance.—Words of Tasso and Socrates.

J. ROUSSEAU, the last of the stick-bearing philosophers, said that the only way to travel was to travel on foot. People do not travel nowadays, for riding from one point to another in a steam-car or a stage-coach is not travelling.

How many have travelled all over the world, and died, alas! without having seen any of its beauties! They have lived in populous cities, have admired monuments erected by the hand of man, have walked in magnificent gardens where all the wonders of creation seemed to be gathered together, but they do not know what a charm there is in following the open road, stick in hand. They know nothing of the broom-bordered paths, the shady forests alive with beautiful birds, the vales, the mountains. They have seen gushing fountains in the city squares, basins and jets in the parks, and great seas and rivers, but they do not know what freshness and harmony is to be found beside the little streams, and the cascades that flow down the rocks.

Every man should, at least once in the course of his life, make a journey of several months on foot, stick in hand. It would be the very hygiene for both body and mind.

But since people no longer travel, the stick has lost much of its old prestige; and we, forgetful of its past glories, look upon it with indifference. The ancients, who seldom travelled except on foot, had a sort of veneration for their stick; they regarded it as a gift from the immortal gods.

Had not most of the gods journeyed over the earth stick in hand? Janus, the guardian of the gates, carries a stick as his symbol. Ceres is frequently represented with this emblem of her journeyings, when she travelled with Triptolemus to teach men the art of agriculture.

Silenus, who accompanied Bacchus in his journeys, is also represented with a stick. History relates that returning from the Indies, these two joyous companions were so well received by a prince through whose states they were travelling, that Bacchus promised to grant him any favor

18

that he might ask. The prince reflected a moment, and as he was not more sensible than ordinary mortals, said :

"I desire that everything I touch may turn to gold."

Bacchus pitied him, but granted his request, and the prince soon possessed as much gold as he could desire.

One day, wishing to entertain the principal personages of his court, he ordered a great feast, and gold being abundant, no expense was spared.

At the dinner hour he merrily took his place, surrounded by his astonished courtiers. His happy guests were enjoying the delicate meats and generous wines; he touched a piece of bread and it was immediately transformed into gold; he took a partridge, it was a golden partridge; he tried to drink, and the wine, as it touched his lips, turned to liquid gold. He rose in dismay to leave the table—he seized his stick, but his hand could not lift it—it had become a heavy bar of gold.

The unhappy king, in the midst of his riches, comprehending the depth of his misery, entreated Bacchus to forgive him for having wished for gold.

" I forgive thee," said Bacchus, "but remember that gold is the most fatal gift that the gods can bestow on mortals."

Cato said he repented of three things : of having spent a single day without learning something, of having confided his secret to a woman, and of having ridden when he might have walked—as he regarded as instructive and useful only the walk with the stick.

> Voyager à bâton, quel plaisir on y goûte !
> Toujours nouveaux objets s'offrent sur votre route ;
> Chaque pas vous présente un spectacle inconnu ;
> On ne revoit jamais ce qu'on a déjà vu.
>
> .   .   .   .
>
> .   .   .   .
>
> Ajoutons qu'on ne peut s'ennuyer nulle part,
> Un lieu vous plaît, on reste ; il vous déplaît, on part.

The fact is we travel too fast, we are always in too great a hurry, and that is why the journey of life is so short. "It is better to hasten at the start than on the road," said a wise man. "Travelling with open eyes is better than studying books," says another. When Tasso had nearly completed his "Jerusalem Delivered," he said he must travel to get some new ideas.

When the poisoned cup was presented to Socrates, raising his eyes to heaven, he said: "O gods, who call me, grant me a happy journey!"

Socrates reminds me of the philosophers' stick.

CHAPTER IV.

THE PHILOSOPHERS' STICK.

*Why are the philosophers represented with a wallet and a long stick?
— Why that wallet?— Why were the philosophers always persecut-
ed?— What is exile?— The citizens of the world.—A thought of
Montaigne.—Of what use is philosophy?—Diogenes and Plato.—
Maxims of Zeno.— What Montesquieu says of him.— Words of
wise men.—Advice of Pittacus to those who wish to marry.—
What distinguishes certain modern philosophers from the ancient
ones.*

THE ancient philosophers are always represented with a wallet and a long stick. Why this wallet? Did it mean that the search for wisdom only made the seekers poor, or did it indicate that true philosophy consists in the disdain for riches?

Both hypotheses are admissible. Those men who made a profession of wisdom and virtue, could but be poor; as soon as some of them became rich, they ceased to be philosophers. But could those be called poor, who did alone, and willingly, what other men only did from necessity? No, since such was their will, and they could dispense with the goods of this world.

When Bias saw the great treasures of Crœsus,

he exclaimed: " How many things that I do not need ! "

This wallet makes me thoughtful, and when I remember that the philosopher Bordas-Desmoulin died poor, and in a miserable garret, I am almost tempted to believe the story that Homer was a beggar.

And why this stick in the hands of the philosophers? It was because, as they so freely spoke truths to the great, they always held themselves ready for exile.

Misfortune follows still—to-day, and always—those who will not pander to the vices and accept the falsehoods of the age; they are accused and condemned by those who hate truth and virtue.

Such was the fate of the philosophers of ancient Greece. As soon as they advanced an opinion contrary to received ideas, or criticised bad laws or bad customs, the anger of the great was unchained against them, and they were doomed to exile.

It was in exile that most of them wrote their immortal works. Very few of them escaped this eternal persecution of the philosopher, this ostracism which always threatened them; therefore it was wise in them to always carry a stick, like travellers about to set out on a journey.

13*

But what is exile? "Am I to believe that the narrow space which confines me, is my only country?" said Anaxagoras, the master of Pericles.

"Nature has given to no man a particular country," said Aristo. "Man is not an earthly plant," said Plato. Socrates said he was neither an Athenian nor a Greek, but a citizen of the world.

The sticks of the philosophers were very long, and as they were always walking, Plutarch calls them "the eternal walkers." This long stick added still more to their naturally grave appearance. And were they not masters, and, as such, were they not entitled to the badge of command?

There was a class of philosophers who carried a stick and wallet, and who were ironically called *Bactroperates.* This scornful epithet was not applied to the disciples of Socrates, but to a number of proud cynics who believed themselves philosphers, because they carried the philosophers' badge.

The real cynics, those of the school of Antisthenes, a disciple of Socrates, seem to have only carried the stick to scourge vice, against which they declared war without distinction of person— so they were the most persecuted. Montaigne has said : " Human wisdom is a double and dangerous sword, and even in the hands of Socrates, its most intimate and familiar friend, how many ends the stick has!"

Aristhenes was asked: "What is the good of thy philosophy?" "It teaches me to live well with myself," replied he. The famous Diogenes wanted to become his disciple, and as Aristhenes rejected him, and threatened him with his stick, "Strike," said the enthusiastic proselyte, "but you will find no stick hard enough to drive me away from you when you speak."

Diogenes exaggerated the philosophy of Aristhenes, but his maxims are no less remarkable. The following is one of them:

"Have good men for thy friends, so that they may encourage thee to do good; and the wicked for enemies, so that they may prevent thee from doing harm."

"What do you do with your stick?" some one asked him one day, as he was warming himself in the sun.

"Drive fools away from me," replied he.

Plato accused Diogenes of pride, and many see nothing in his philosophy but an insult to the human race—but does it not also prove love of independence and scorn for riches? When there are so many men whom the love of greatness makes servile, low, grovelling, we feel that we still have need of the cynics' stick.

Crates, a disciple of Socrates, indignant at the baseness displayed by men in the pursuit of riches, sold his rich patrimony, and threw away the money saying, " I am free."

Athens was the principal rendezvous of these stick-bearers, whose maxims will forever be the rule of philosophy. Zeno, one of the most illustrious among them, said : " The wise man alone is rich ; the wise man is king."

Ah ! I bow before the stick of this wise man—before the sceptre of this king—and when I stand erect again I do not feel humiliated ; I am even proud of my submission.

" In what does knowledge consist ? " asked one of his disciples.

" In being ignorant of what ought not to be known," replied he. This maxim alone would be praise enough for Zeno, if Cato had not proved that the philosophy of the Stoics was right.

" If I could," said Montesquieu, " forget that I am a Christian, I could not help thinking the destruction of the sect of Zeno among the misfortunes of the human race."

Another of Zeno's teachings, the forgetting of which has always been the cause of the downfall

of nations, is : " Private interests should be sacri-
ficed to general interests, and to the safety of the
.State."

It is to the forgetting of this precept that
France owes her downfall—I hardly dare say her
humiliation.

Let us listen to the maxims of these masters,
who, stick in hand, used to teach under the por-
ticos, and in the lyceums.

Thales.—" The wise man is always rich, but it
is very seldom that the rich man is wise."

Salon.—" Judge of what you see by what you
see."

· *Pittacus.*—" Prudence is necessary to foresee
misfortunes, and courage to bear them."

Cleobulus.—" The true way to discourage the
wicked is to praise the good and assist them."

Pythagoras.—" Respect thyself."

Chilon.—" Beware of thyself."

" If these wise maxims had been followed,"
said Bossuet, " the world would have known only
great men and good citizens."

Pittacus of Mytilene, one of whose maxims we
have just quoted, met one of his disciples, who
consulted him on the choice of a wife.

" I have two in view," said the young man ;
" one my equal in means and family connections ;

the other above me in both : which of them do you advise me to marry ?"

Pittacus pointed with his stick to a group of · children playing top. " Look at those children," said he, " and you will understand that you must marry your equal."

> " Le jeune homme voyant que chacun à sa force
>   Mesuroit la grandeur de la toupie au foit,
>   Il connut clairement ce que faire il devoit,
>   Se gardant d'estre pris des grandeurs à l'amorce."

It was after the time of these wise, austere men, that these pretended philosophers, of whom we have just spoken, and who believed that they were imitating their masters because they carried sticks, made their appearance. They wore a very coarse, short woollen tunic, and a large cloak of the same material ; walked with a grave and meas- ured step, and carried a long stick ; and their manner was to imitate Chilon's laconism. To-day this type no longer exists, and what distinguishes our modern philosophers is neither the laconism, nor the dress, nor the stick of the ancients—it is often only their garrulity.

CHAPTER V.

THE PHILOSOPHERS' STICK (CONTINUED).

A few lines of moralizing.—Aristotle and the young Indian woman.—Why the Greeks were subdued by the Romans.—Where Aristhenes proves that every man thinks himself fit to command. —The love of the Stick, that is, of command.—The noblest and least envied of the Sticks.—Why Denis, king, became a schoolmaster.—How, in olden time, the Iliad and the Odyssey were taught.—The sceptre-ferule.

E designedly enlarged in the preceding chapter on the doctrines of the ancient philosophers, and even should the reader accuse us of pedagogism, we will still devote a few lines to this science, which teaches man his duties in prescribing for him a wise conduct, and in enabling him to conform his actions thereto. And yet this science taught by the stick-bearing ancients has always had its detractors; for it is hard to make people admit that the maxims of the laical philosophers of Greece and Rome are the foundation of the evangelical doctrines.

Aristotle, at whose expense people have made too merry, has above all others incurred the reprobation of the wise men of our time ; and yet Alexander said of him, " I have conquered fewer people with my sceptre than Aristotle with his stick."

A young and very beautiful Indian woman resolved to insnare Aristotle. With this intention she went to him, and played her part so well that the philosopher who was walking alone in his garden, dropped his stick and threw himself at the feet of the beautiful slave. The young woman seemed to be on the point of acceding to this transport, but, oh, the capriciousness of love !—she must make a condition.

" Command, and I will obey," sighs the philosopher.

They are in a dense shade, where no human eye can penetrate—even the sun would try in vain to throw an indiscreet ray into the mysterious reduct.

The woman, after timidly hesitating, said, " I would like to ride on your back."

The request is absurd—foolish—but the philosopher is more foolish still. He gets down on all fours (says the author of this ridiculous story), and the woman, who has picked up the philosopher's stick, places herself upon his back, and strikes him as she would an old horse.

THE STICK AND THE STOIC.

Suddenly a burst of laughter is heard behind a clump of trees—it is Alexander, his pupil, who has come to take a lesson of him who is called the acme of human perfection.

Were this story, gotten up to prove that his practice did not quite accord with his teaching, true, it would not tarnish the memory of this illustrious stick-bearer.

When the true philosophy ceased to reign in Greece, she was soon subjugated by the Romans; and subjugation is the fate reserved for every power which has become degenerate by false pride, false knowledge, false virtue, and too many would-be leaders.

Antisthenes said that in olden time it was hard to find seven sages in Greece, and that at the same time it would have been hard to find seven men who did not deem themselves worthy to be stick-bearers. Is not this the same Antisthenes who said, that if in the amphitheatre of Athens all the citizens of one profession had been told to rise, and the others to remain seated, this order would have been very readily obeyed; but if the same order had been given to all those who thought themselves competent to regulate great affairs, or to govern a republic, no one would have remained seated.

14

Alas. may not the same be said of Frenchmen to-day?

In France, where the love of independence is so deep rooted, every one aspires more or less to command, and every man professes a holy horror for the stick, unless he carries it himself. Strange inconsistency! And here is another inconsistency —but this among princes.

As soon as they obtain the sceptre, they think themselves irremovable; they are very willing the people should have the privilege of giving it to them, but they deny them the right to take it from them; and if it is taken from them, they foment civil or foreign wars to recover its possession.

To return to the philosophers. There are among them masters, who like kings enjoyed absolute power, and used it like despots, with no fear of overturned thrones and broken sticks of command. These were the schoolmasters. No sceptre was more noble nor less envied than theirs.

I respectfully bow before these sovereigns who have made war on ignorance only, on the battle-ground of our schools.

I would have the holy function of teaching become so honorable, that the name of teacher

would be the highest title that could be conferred
on man.

Cicero, the worthy interpreter of the moral
philosophy of Greece, said that if Denis, king, and
then teacher, had in his misfortune selected the
latter profession, it was so as not to lose the habit
of command. I prefer to think, it was out of love
for the philosophy with which Plato had inspired
him.

Some one asked him, "Of what use have the
teachings of this master been to you?"

"They have taught me to bear my disgrace,"
replied he.

The schoolmasters of those days used two sticks
for teaching; a red one for the Iliad, and a yel-
low one for the Odyssey.

Gradually the stick was used more to punish
than to teach, and the more flexible wood of the
ferule was adopted, as being better adapted to
the new employment for which the emblem was
intended.

Teaching and the ferule have long been inseparable. It was an old prejudice, that teaching
could only be done with the assistance of blows
with the ferule.

Theodoric, king of the Goths, forbade his warriors to send their children to school, "because," said

he, " they can not but fear the sword, after having
feared the ferule." It would have been much
simpler to suppress the ferule, but it was a prejudice ; and it requires ages to outgrow prejudices,
no matter how foolish they are.

In the lower empire the ferule was called
sceptre ; hence the name ferule-bearer, by which
the princes of that day were known.

The revolution of 1789 forgot to break the
sceptre-ferule, but since then good sense has done
it that justice.

We have abolished the ferule as unnecessary
in the education of children, and perhaps the day
will come, when all nations will abolish the sceptre as unnecessary to the happiness of men.

CHAPTER VI.

THE STICK AS A WEAPON OF WAR.

*The Stick according to Ducange.—The charters and other exam-
ples taken from the life of Bayard and Nostradamus.—How
fighting was done before the days of powder.—How the Canadians
fought.—The arms of the ancient Germans.—What the German
arms were formerly called.—The wars of 1870-71.—Are the
Germans of to-day more civilized than those of old?—Which of
them better deserve the name of barbarians?—Where is courage
to-day?—Where is humanity?—Where is civilization?*

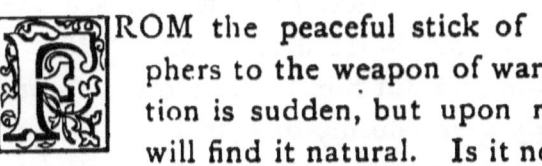ROM the peaceful stick of the philoso-
phers to the weapon of war, the transi-
tion is sudden, but upon reflection we
will find it natural. Is it not really the
nature of the stick to sometimes thus pass suddenly from the passive to the active state?

The word stick at first awakens in the mind only
the idea of its habitual use, but it was not so with
our fathers. They gave this name to all sorts of
arms, even to guns. Thus to say armed, in no matter what way, they said *embastonné* or *abastonné*.

Duconge gives us many examples of this.

"They were *bastonnés* with swords, lances, and
other sticks."

14*

Charter of 1465: " Embastonnés with swords, and other invasive arms."

For disarm they said *débastonner.*

Charter of 1449: " This Huart was débastonné of his sword-cane."

" This varlet watched the prior being *débastonné* of a sword which he had, and came and struck the said prior on the head."

Here is another example from the life of Bayard :

" Master friend," said the young page Bayard to the head groom of the Duke de Savoie, " I heard the king tell my lord that he wants to see me, mounted on my old horse after dinner. If you will groom him and put him in good order for me I will willingly give you my dagger."

The master-groom, pleased with the boy's generosity, said :

" Bayard, my friend, keep your stick. I don't want it."

Pierre de Bayard was at that time only a novice in arms, but his stick had already accomplished many feats of prowess.

Nostradamus, in his *Histoire de Provence* also gives the name of stick to all sorts of arms.

" Here are fifteen or twenty cheveliers armed with crossbows and other sticks."

We want to prove by these examples that the conquerors of the stick are numerous, and that this eternal accomplice of human wickedness has always been true to its origin, for under a thousand different forms of warlike arms, it has always borne its old name.

It may be said, that before the fatal invention of powder, men only made war with the stick.

" They fought with nails, and fists, and sticks, and finally with the arms that were afterwards manufactured."

I find in the *Singularités de la France Antarctique :*

The Canadians fought with round arrows, clubs, square sticks, lances, and wooden pikes pointed with bone instead of iron. They fought like savages with their fists and teeth, and even pulled each others' hair. Herodotus in his fourth book speaks of certain nations who fought with sticks, and says besides that the virgins of that country were in the habit of fighting every year with sticks in honor of Minerva. Diodorus, in his first book, says that Hercules was compelled to fight with clubs, for at that time there were no other arms in use. By referring to Plutarch, Justin, and other authors, it will be seen that the Romans fought naked, and that the Thebans and the

Lacedemonians fought with handspikes and big sticks.

The principal arm of the Romans was a short stick with a sharp iron point, and it might properly be said, that this is the stick that conquered the world. The fall of the Gauls before the Roman armies, must be attributed to this terrible pike.

The Gauls fought with long, double-edged swords rounded at the end, so that they could not stab. Relying upon the sharpness of their blades, they struck so as to cut the sticks of the Romans. But the hard wood of the Roman weapon resisted the blow, and the swords of the Gauls were broken or bent against them, says Kalybius. Then while the Gallic soldier stooped to try to straighten his sword, the Roman fell upon him and stabbed him with his pike.

Neither the Franks, the Goths, nor any of the Germans knew much about iron. Until the sixth century, the only arms that these people had was the stick proper and the club. Their war arm was given them in public assembly, and they considered it such an honor to carry their war stick, that they never appeared in the temples or at festivals without it. It was unlawful to either give it away, or lend it, even to save one's life. Those who lost it, were dishonored. The greatest disgrace to a German soldier was to have his stick taken from him.

The Germans long fought with sticks and clubs, and for that reason, in their ancient history, their army is called *Knuddaheer*. *Knobs* is an old Belgian word signifying club.

See those warriors, covered with an ox-skin and armed with their terrible stick of war! Ferocity is written on their faces—everything about them indicates barbarity, their restless eyes, their thin lips, their steaming nostrils, like those of a furious bull ready to rush into the arena.

Such were, thirteen centuries ago, the formidable warriors whom everybody agrees were barbarians, and who—the war of 1870–71, between the French and Germans, has just proved it—were less barbarous than those of to-day.

The barbarians of old, far from burning villages and pillaging houses, forbade their soldiers, under terrible penalties, to destroy or march over sowed fields. If a slave stole only a sheep from a countryman, he forfeited his hand; if a gentleman, he was only compelled to return it; but if a free man, he paid besides a fine of fifty rolo. Incendiaries were deprived of their sticks, and dismissed the camp forever. Those convicted of intoxication, were allowed nothing but water to drink for a certain length of time. Women who followed the army were punished by having their noses cut off.

The following order was issued by Theodoric, king of the Goths, to a corps of Gepides whom he sent to reinforce the Gauls :

"To make your march victorious, let it be marched with moderation, and conduct yourselves like men devoted to the public good. Do not wrong those who are not armed, and be generous to the vanquished foe. Never stain your sticks with innocent blood. Inflict no injury on those of your own side, and do not bring ruin on those whom you go to defend."

Which of the two, the ancients or the moderns, deserve the name of barbarians?

These wars of stick and club called for true courage. The combatants fought with eyes, voice, man to man, body to body. The more skill, strength, and coolness a warrior possessed, the sooner he could overthrow his enemy.

The enemy overthrown or disarmed, the battle ceased, and the vanquished were sure of the magnanimity of the victors.

To-day, when war is only a mathematical problem, when the needle-gun and the Krupp cannon have displaced the stick and the club—when an invisible enemy is fought without passion : coldly, stupidly, even—when the most cowardly may kill the most courageous—the feeblest the strongest—the least adroit the most skillful; to-day, when like thunder, death strikes at random, piling upon the battle-field thousands of dead and dying,—where is courage? where is humanity?

And it is after so many centuries of social progress that people reflect more than ever on these hideous wars which are the negation of civilization.

He will be the friend of humanity who will annihilate all implements of war, and prevent the manufacture of new ones. A race of soldiers becomes terribly barbarous.

CHAPTER VII.

VILLAIN AND STICK.

The origin of the point of honor according to Montesquieu.—How gentlemen used to fight.—The difference between a blow and a slap.—Repressive laws against clubbing

THE stick was destined to be simultaneously the representation of the two extreme points of social life. If it is an emblem of glory and an instrument of despotism, it is, at the same time, an emblem of shame and an instrument of humiliation.

Starting from this principle, Montesquieu wrote concerning the stick his celebrated chapter of *l'Esprit des lois* called " Origin of the point of honor."

"We find," said he, " enigmas in the codes of the barbarians. The laws of the Frisons only allowed a half cent of composition to him who had received blows with a stick, and for the smallest wound more is given.

In the Salic law, if a free man gave another free man blows with a stick, he was fined three cents ; if he had drawn blood, he was punished as if he had stabbed with iron, and fined fifteen cents. The fine was proportioned to the size of the wound. The law of the Lombards established different compositions for one, two, three, or four blows. To-day one blow is worth a thousand.

This law of the Lombards, inserted in the constitution of Charlemagne, compels those whom it permits to fight duels, to fight only with the stick.

The capitulary of Louis the Wild allows the choice of the stick or other arms, but afterwards there were serfs who only fought with the stick. One law of Frederick the First forbade the wearing of the sword by commoners; the simple and naked stick alone was allowed them. Lalouette complained that in his time (the seventeenth century), the law was no longer observed; and he regarded it as a great mistake.

Gentlemen fought each other on horseback and with their weapons, and villains fought on foot and with the stick. Thence it followed that the stick was an instrument of outrage, because a man who had been struck with it had been treated like a villain.

Only villains fought with uncovered faces, so only they could receive blows on the face. A

15

slap in the face was an insult which had to be
washed in blood, because the man who received
it was treated like a villain.

Those lines from l'Esprit des lois remind me of
an adventure of Mgr. de Talleyrand-Périgord,
bishop of Autun.

One day, as he was in angry discussion with
Fouché, whom it was said he had denounced, the
latter gave him a superb slap in the face.

"Oh, the brute! *what a blow!*" exclaimed
Talleyrand.

That was the cunning diplomat's way of elud-
ing the point of honor.   A blow was not an outrage which demanded blood, like a slap in the face
or a blow with a stick.

French legislation has always busied itself much
with the stick.   One of the rules of the marshals
of France, of the 22d of August, 1858, says :
" For blows with a stick the offender shall be imprisoned a whole year, and this time can be shortened by six months only, by the payment of
three thousand livres to the hospital nearest the
home of the injured party."   Besides that, the
striker was obliged to go down on his knees and
ask the forgiveness of the injured party, who had
a right to give him in return as many blows as
he had received from him.   If he was too gener-

ous to do this, the judge had the power to compel him to do it.

Another rule is, that the one who administers blows with a stick, after having received a slap or other blows with the hand, is condemned to two years imprisonment, and to four, if he was not struck first.

In our time, blows are not often taken to court. Many journalists have received them, and have nevertheless remained very honorable men, without even having washed away the insult in blood, which washing in blood is rather an idiotic kind of revenge, for there is no telling whose blood will be spilled. All writers are not anxious to have their brains scattered, or their breasts perforated, because some fool who thinks a pen has insulted him, will only reply with a stick.

CHAPTER VIII.

DUELLING.

Duelling in England.—A duel under Pharamond.—Inconsistency of Henry IV. and Louis XIV.—How duels are fought in the Kurile Isles.—Means recommended for the prevention of duelling. —The only way to make it absolutely impossible.

T is in vain that philosophers and moralists say and write, that the practice of duelling is absurd; that the point of honor attached to it is a prejudice worthy of a still barbarous people; that good sense disapproves of it, and reason condemns it: nothing up to the present time, not even the law against it, has been of any avail—the foolish custom will not be suppressed. Because, slaves of prejudice that we are, we would consider ourselves dishonored if we did not give the man who has insulted us the privilege of killing us.

In England, where fist and club fighting are lawful amusements, duelling, properly so called, is very rare to-day. This is because the English law, instead of recurring like our French law to subtile analogies to reach the duellists, strikes directly at duelling as an act of felony ; it not only condemns it, but it dishonors the duellist, assimilating him with malefactors and vagabonds.

In France, on the contrary, we honor the name of the brave challenger, and we brand as a coward the one who refuses to fight.

Helvetius relates, that Pharamond having upbraided one of his soldiers for having disobeyed his orders by fighting a duel, the latter said to him :

"Why should I obey your orders? You only punish with imprisonment those who violate them, but you punish with infamy those who obey them."

The same answer might have been given to Henry IV., who made laws against duelling, and treated with contempt those who obeyed them.

Louis XIV. was still more inconsistent ; he issued an edict of death against duellists, and at the same time granted letters patent to fencing masters.

The sanction of the church and the law in authorizing judiciary contests, in which the villain was only allowed the use of the stick, has contributed much to perpetuate the mania for duelling. Duel masses were celebrated in those days, *pro duello*.

15*

In the Kurile Isles, which are a dependency of Kamschatka, they have a way of fighting duels which I would like to see introduced into our customs.

The challenger first receives three hard blows with a stick on his back; then he returns them to his adversary, and this game is continued until one of the duellists either sues for mercy, or dies under the blows. This should be tried with us— it would perhaps prevent duelling.

Another means worthy of trial, is that employed by some king—I have forgotten whom. In spite of the laws which he had made against it, two officers of high rank went to him one day, to beg leave to fight a duel. The prince was offended at the request, but concealed his resentment.

" I consent," replied he, " but I will be present at the fight, and will appoint the time and place."

This was agreed to.

At the appointed hour the prince arrived on the ground, accompanied by his guards. He sent for the executioner, and said to him:

" My friend, as soon as one of them is killed, cut off the head of the other right here in my presence."

At these words the two officers stood motionless; then throwing themselves at the king's feet, they entreated his forgiveness. After that he heard no more of duelling.

History tells us what means Marshal de Brissac used to stop duelling. He ordered that duels should be fought on a bridge between four pikes, that the vanquished party should be thrown into the river, and that his adversary should make no attempt to save him.

Since laws can not stop duelling, it should be made impossible. But how? Thus:

One of my friends was challenged one day. He had the choice of weapons, luckily for him, for his adversary could put a ball in a two-cent piece at twenty paces; he was also a good swordsman, while my friend had never learned to fence except with the stick.

"What weapon do you choose?" asked the seconds.

My friend reflected a moment; then said:

" I choose the stick."

" That is too mean a weapon," remarked a witness; " why not choose the sabre?"

" Well, the sabre, then," replied my friend · " the sword, if you prefer it; but on one condition: it is that we fight at twenty paces."

They supposed he was joking, but he was quite

in earnest; he would either have the stick or the sabre at twenty paces.

It is easy to imagine that the duel did not take place.

This queer method is certainly the best to recommend.

Duelling with any weapon whatsoever, being based upon the right of the strongest, is contrary to the laws of justice; and yet nothing has been able to prevent it, because there still remains in our society an aftergrowth of the old feudal custom, which consists in taking the law into one's own hands.

———

CHAPTER IX.

THE ART OF THE STICK.

The science of the Stick.—The aphorisms of a cudgeller.—The empire of the Stick.—The Decembraillards.—The society of the United Cudgellers.—How many blows with a stick can be given in thirty seconds.—A celebrated and inoffensive stick.

 REMEMBER an armory of the *quartier Latin* that was very much frequented in 184-, where the art of using the cudgel was especially taught. There were a dozen of us, students, who were almost passionately fond of this kind of fencing.

The name of our fencing-master was Gousset. He was a very strong man, most devilishly irritable, much feared by his equals, but withal a good fellow, and very talkative—especially when we invited him to drink.

"Gentlemen," he often said to us, "learn how to use the stick with one or both hands—then I will answer for you. In no matter what situation you may find yourselves, no matter how many enemies you may have, you can victoriously repulse their attacks, with this weapon in your hands." "Why," he sometimes said, as he twirled his stick, "with this instrument, I could repulse a squad of policemen." Gousset was a fanatic on the stick question. "Fencing with the stick," he also said, "develops the body more than any other exercise. It is the best way to acquire strength and suppleness. After six months of this healthful exercise, you will be proof against diseases of the chest."

Gousset's aphorisms on this subject occur to me :

"The knowledge of the stick is the knowledge of life."

"Aim at the breast, but strike at the head."

"Beware of your own eyes ; let no one know where you are going to strike."

"Man is only successful through audacity. Be expert with the stick, and you will be audacious."

"Have confidence in your stick, and you will have confidence in yourself."

"To be feared is better than to be loved ; and nothing inspires fear so much as a good, solid stick."

"We ought to know how to use the stick, and how to shake hands."

These aphorisms of Gousset seem to have been put in practice principally by a celebrated society formed in 1850, and which was christened by the public *Decembraillards.*

"The organization of this society was formid-able," says M. Ernest Hamel, in his patriotic *Histoire du second Empire.* It was a whole army recruited from the soldiers, and men of no pro-fession or trade, who were ready for anything. Its members were armed with long, iron-pointed sticks, which they were always ready to use on those who were not as enthusiastic as they.

It was on the plain of Satory, near Versailles, on the 10th of October, 1850, that the *Decem-braillards* appeared for the first time, armed with their clubs. They were reviewed by Louis Na-poleon, at that time president of the republic.

On that day the aphorism of our master, Gous-set, was realized. "You should know how to strike with a club, and how to shake hands." Here the hand-shakings were bottles of wine dis-tributed among the soldiers.

"When," said an eye witness, " partisans of the new empire were seen exciting the enthusiasm of the troops, and provoking the cries of ' Vive l'Empereur!'" a bottle in one hand, and a club in the other.

And the empire arose ! ! !

In 1869, when this power which M. de la Gueronnière called in a journal the *club empire*, was about to fall, the stick again tried to play its political part.

Unfortunately for the men who still dream of the feudal stick, the people of to-day no longer allow themselves to be cudgelled, and the society of the cudgellers had its trouble for its pains.

And the empire fell ! ! !

It is the fate reserved to all nations whose principle is not *The Right*, that they can only rise and be maintained by force.

If, in all ages and with all nations, cudgelling has been practiced—as we shall see it has, in the next book of this history—it belonged to our epoch to make an art of this practice. But happily for our generation, this art is only exercised to-day in a platonic way, although there are still backs ready to bend before the first stick that comes along.

In Gousset's time only forty to fifty blows were given in thirty seconds. Our cudgellers of to-day can administer from seventy to eighty.

Such progress in the art of cudgelling makes me muse !

To all cudgellers, past, present, and to come— to all stick-bearers, kings, emperors, or prelates, I prefer the inoffensive cudgeller who lately per-

formed tricks with his stick on the Place de la
Madeline, and on the great boulevards, and whom
all Paris has seen throw in the air, with the end
of his stick, a small coin which always fell into
his vest pocket, amid the deafening shouts of the
people. This cudgel-player modestly called himself the first stick-juggler of Europe.

We can forgive him for this feeling of pride, for
his stick never tyrannized over nor hurt any one.
It knew how to command respect without inspiring
fear.

BOOK FIFTH.

PUNISHMENT BY THE STICK.

CHAPTER I.

THE BASTINADO.

The bastinado among the Jews.—The threat of Rehoboam.—The holy martyr Eleazar.—An edict of Ptolemy Philapator.—The tympanum.—The Cross.—The bastinado among the Romans.—The Centurion.—The grape-vine.

BATON (stick), which was formerly written *baston,* whence comes, *bastonnade* (bastinado), and which comes from *batuo, batuis,* which signifies *battre* (to beat), has justified its etymology in being used specially to strike (frapper), a word derived from the Greek which means *bâton* (stick).

All the old legislations have used this instrument, predestined as a means of punishment. After having been the first representative of authority it became the first representative of penal law. So it was the first punishment that was ever inflicted on man, slave or free.

This punishment, which was generally called bastinado, and which before 1785 was still in use in France, in the army and navy—except for gentlemen soldiers, be it understood—would be disgraceful to-day.

Another of the prerogatives of the stick gone with the old régime!

In our day, if we want to witness this shameful punishment, we shall have to go to China, Turkey, Russia, or Germany; everywhere, in fact, where feudalism still reigns.

And it is because punishment by the stick is disappearing before the progress of universal civilization, that we wish to devote a few pages to it.

The Jews were formerly the most ferocious cudgellers in the world. Sometimes they made the instrument of punishment more attractive by ornamenting it with points and thorns.

" My father chastised you with whips, but I will chastise you with scorpions," said Rehoboam, king of the Hebrews, to his people, who begged him to lighten the yoke which his father had put upon them.

The bastinado was so well suited to the tastes of the Israelites, and they were so willing to use it, that Moses forbade them to administer more than forty blows; but as the law only limited the quantity, and said nothing of the quality, it often followed that the patient expired at the thirty-fifth.

This punishment was the one most in use, doubtless because it was the quickest, and demanded the least preparation.

We see in the third book of Maccabees that Ptolemy Philapator, having taken Jerusalem, ordered his generals to lead the Jews into captivity, and issued the following edict: "Whoever shall conceal a Jew, young or old, shall be beaten to death, and all his family with him."

When the Romans had subdued the ancient kingdoms of Judea and Israel, they took away from the Jews the right of life and death of criminals, and only allowed them to administer twenty-five blows with their favorite instrument.

What we call bastinado, the Israelites called tympanum, whence comes tympanize to beat the skin—of a drum. A better figure could not have been found.

Saint Paul says that the holy martyr Eleazar would not ransom himself from the tympanum, because he hoped for a happier resurrection.

Jesus also was condemned to suffer that infamous punishment, for speaking the truth too plainly to the Jews.

The title of Roman citizen gave exemption from the bastinado. Cicero said it was a sin to chain a Roman citizen, but a crime to strike him ; it was lawful, however, to bastinade condemned prisoners, so that by this ignominious punishment they might lose their title of citizen.

The bastinado was an infamous punishment, used only in the armies. If the offense was trifling, the offender only received a few blows. For hired soldiers, the stick was made of the wood of which the ferule is made ; for the Roman soldiers, grape-vine was used. The hired soldiers received their punishment from the Romans ; the Romans from the Centurion.

The Centurion always carried this instrument of punishment in his hand ; indeed it was so inseparable from this estimable functionary, that in inscriptions the stick is used to represent the Centurion—is substituted for the word. It was a twig of grape-vine, bent at the upper extremity, and was only used when the bastinado was not intended to kill. There was less dishonor attached to it than to any other stick.

The vine has always had strange immunities !

The bastinado changed its name when applied

16*

to soldiers condemned to death ; it was then called *fustuarium,* and was continued until death followed.*

According to Kalybius, the punishment was inflicted not only upon officers and deserters, but also upon those who boasted of a heroic act which they had not performed.

---

* Kalybius thus explains this military punishment : " The military council is assembled, and the tribune presides ; if the accused is condemned, the tribune takes a cane with which he lightly strikes the culprit ; the legionary soldiers instantly fall upon him, and beat him to death. Sometimes the culprit does not die, but it would be as well for him if he did, for he is never allowed to reappear in public, and no one, not even parents or relatives, dare shelter him. A man who has suffered this torture is looked upon as dead."

CHAPTER II.

AMONG THE CHINESE.

The Stick in China.—A Chinese tribunal.—Sentence and punishment.—The twenty thousand Mandarins.—How imprudent it is to advise a son of the sun.—The horse of the kings of Tsi.—Freedom of the press in China.—The stamping of the book.—How to escape the bastinado.—An article of the penal code of the Chinese.—We must not despair of the times.

F the stick is used by the different nations of the earth for different purposes, it may be said that with them all, it has always been one of the commonest means of correction. It would seem that God, in creating the human race, condemned it to the punishment of the stick.

This instrument of arbitrariness and justice has been, and always will be, most used in China. There all punishments begin with the bastinado. There are none among the inhabitants who have not suffered it at least once. No one is secure from it, not even the mandarin of the highest rank, which fact made a missionary say, and with great truth, that the stick governs in China.

For some time past, however, legislation has been introducing noted modifications in this practice. When the judge orders five blows, the criminal only receives four, according to that Chinese axiom, which is not to be disdained: "When laws are made, rigor is necessary; when they are executed, mercy is no less so."

A grave mandarin is seated. Before him is a table on which lie a dozen canes. Like the Roman duumvir, he has behind him his implacable lictors, armed with bamboos or sticks.

The criminal awaits his sentence, for which the judge is not compelled to give his reasons. If the accused is guilty, and according to the degree of his guilt, he, the judge, throws on the ground a certain number of the sticks placed before him. The officers immediately seize the culprit, turn down his trousers, and conscientiously administer to him five blows for each stick thrown down. There is a change of executioners after every five blows; or rather, two executioners strike alternately, so that the blows may be heavier, and the punishment greater.

When the offense is light, the mandarin gives the criminal the privilege of hiring some one to take his punishment. In that fantastical country it is quite a common thing to see at the door of

THE STICK IN FAR CATHAY—JAPANESE CEREMONIAL.

the tribunals, men who make a business of receiving the bastinado for others.

After his punishment, the patient is compelled to kneel, to touch the ground three times with his forehead, and to thank both the mandarin, his judge, and the lictors (who licked him) who carried out the sentence. In the great tribunals this condemnation is sometimes equivalent to the sentence of death. It is hardly necessary to administer more than a hundred blows to send a son of the Celestial Empire on his everlasting journey.

A mandarin never goes out without being accompanied by his lictors. If any one forgets to kneel as he passes, he may depend upon it that five or six blows, nimbly applied by the lictors, will punish him for his absent-mindedness.

It is easy to imagine the number of sticks that constantly hang over the backs of these children of the sun, when it is remembered that in this empire there are no less than twenty thousand civil mandarins.

China is the only country in the world where the stick takes precedence of the sword. A civil mandarin enjoys a much greater degree of consideration than a military one. The latter often walks, sometimes rides on horseback; while the

former never goes out except in a chaise borne
by four men.

The emperor himself, although he is called the son
of heaven, never goes out without holding in his
hand the traditional instrument of Chinese justice ;
and perhaps to set a good example, he often uses it.

Although he is the most absolute despot of the
earth, he has his council of state; but if a councillor,
no matter how high his rank, gives any advice, or
offers any suggestion which does not please him,
the celestial monarch gives him in return a sound
thrashing.   Yet for all that, there are councillors
whom the fear of the stick has not deterred from
remonstrating with the emperor.   The following
example will prove it:

Kin-Kong, king of Tsi, had a horse which he
prized very highly.   This horse died through the
fault of his keeper.   The king, on hearing the sad
news, rushed at the groom with a raised stick,
but one of his ministers, seeing his anger, stopped
his arm.

" What are you going to do ? " said he cour-
ageously to his sovereign.   " Would you strike
that man before telling him how great a fault he
has committed ? "

" Well, you tell him, and let him prepare to
receive a hundred blows."

So the minister said to the groom : " Miserable wretch, listen attentively while I tell you of what crimes you are guilty: in the first place you have been the cause of the death of this horse that the prince had confided to your care ; this offense deserves death. In the second place, it is your fault that my prince, after having lost his horse, lost his temper, and became angry enough to strike you ; that is a second crime even greater than the first. And finally, all the princes and all the neighboring states will know that my prince has killed a man to avenge the death of a horse. His reputation will be ruined, and it is all thy fault ; thou art the cause of it all ! '

" Let him go," said the king. " I forgive him."

There is perfect freedom of the press in China, only it is well for men of letters to remember and observe the maxim of Figaro : " Say nothing against any person nor any thing." Whoever indulges in the least bit of satire, or publishes an uncertain item of news, is summoned before the mandarin and sentenced to receive the bastinado. After the punishment has been inflicted, the objectionable article is allowed to circulate freely all over the empire of the sun. The stick is the stamp of the book, which the author receives on his back.

If the number of blows does not exceed twenty —for any offense whatsoever—they leave no mark, and are regarded as a fatherly correction.

As is the case in every feudal government, the Chinese law opens a wide door to arbitrariness, and its worthy auxiliary, the stick, as will be seen by this article of the penal code :

" Whoever is guilty of conduct unbecoming, and contrary to the *spirit of the laws*, without, however, having violated any especial article, will be liable to receive at least forty blows ; but if the *impropriety is of a grave nature*, he shall receive eighty blows."

By means of this ambiguous definition, a magistrate has it in his power to administer any number of blows. The poor Chinese can make no complaint, for the inevitable stick is always ready for those who dare demand justice, to teach them not to importune the court.

At the commencement of our history, the clergy obeyed a somewhat similar law.

The third article of a capitulary of Pepin the Short, in the year 755, says that any priest or monk who shall dare to make a complaint against his bishop, shall be punished with the bastinado.

In our day civilization, which began in the West, tends to the subjugation of all the Asiatic nations to its humanitarian yoke. It will also conquer China. This people, who for ninety-six million years--according to its annals—has submitted with resignation to this paternal *régime* of the stick, has even begun its little social revolution.

We must not despair of the future.

CHAPTER III.

THE GREAT JUSTICIARY.

The beau ideal of an absolute government.—Turkish justice.—What return the bastinado makes to a judge.—Islamism and civilization.—Father Lobo in Abyssinia.—Knout and battock in Russia.—An adventure of Mourawief.—Marriage by the stick.—The force of habit.—Ignorance and slavery in America.—The Stick saves from death.

IT is impossible to examine the history of ancient and modern legislation without finding that the stick is everywhere the principal instrument of torture, and the great justiciary of nations; so we will continue to review its acts among the different nations.

We will begin with Turkey.

17

This country is under such subjection to the stick,—that is to say, to absolute power, of which its government is the beau ideal,—that from the grand vizier to the pacha, everyone possessing any authority is allowed to use the stick as much as he pleases.

Even the grand mistress of the harem carries a stick, as a symbol of her power, and the white shoulders of the odalisques are not always exempt from its blows.

The laws of the Turks, like those of the Chinese, have preserved the traditional stick, and it is there considered the most efficacious of punishments. The only difference is that in Turkey the punishment is less general and swifter. *Turkish justice* has become proverbial; it never keeps litigants in suspense. The pacha orders them to be beaten on the soles of the feet, and sends them home. This manner of proceeding keeps alive fear, the best auxiliary of the stick.*

The Turks have always been distinguished for

---

* If the stick has in all times been the symbol of Power, it has also and more especially been the symbol of Fear. In like manner, if it is the synonym of command, it is also the synonym of slavery. The Pagans building temples to the Furies, who were armed with whips, shows how much power Fear has always had over the feeble minds of mortals. Does not Xerxes, throwing chains into the sea and proudly striking the waves with his stick, seem to express that chain and stick are also synonyms?

THE STICK IN THE SERAGLIO.

their anti-social dispositions. They are naturally cruel in their punishments. The Sultana calls her son, my lion (azslanem), or my tiger (caplanem). This shows the barbarous instincts of the people. A writer in the beginning of this century thus describes the bastinado in the Ottoman Empire:

The culprit is tied to the stake head downwards; he is beaten on his feet and his back, and sometimes receives five hundred blows. The judge is present at the execution of the sentence, and counts on his rosary the number of blows. After the punishment is over, he is paid for his trouble a dollar (piastre) for each blow.

It is bad for the culprit when the judge is covetuous, and it is well known that cupidity is not the least conspicuous of the Turks' characteristics. The love of money and the love of the stick have destroyed his ideas of human dignity, and he has no more regard for honor than for the life of a criminal.

We are bound to say, however, that for the last thirty years the Ottoman Empire has been tending to free itself from the degrading *régime* which for so many centuries has composed its penal code. But how much longer will it be before the idea of emancipation which is fomenting in Europe will at last deliver Turkey from the odious yoke of the grand viziers and the pachas? Alas! perhaps it will never be. The problem of its regeneration is insoluble. There is a wide abyss between Islamism and Western civilization.

If Russia should one day take Constantinople, the Turks would only have changed sticks.

What a fine country the East is for the profession of the monarch. To enjoy unlimited authority, to exercise a tyranny that nothing can legally restrain ; to be master of the life and the property of his subjects ; to inspire, even in his courtiers and ministers, terror and veneration ; and to have no fear, like the monarchs of the West, that a social revolution will break their sceptre ! Is not that the ideal of royalty?

And they enjoy many other privileges ; personages of high rank fill their harems with beautiful women, and no one ever thinks of criticising their acts, or would dare to look through the wall of their private lives.

Every man who is admitted to the presence of royalty must kneel as if in the Divine presence.

Have I not good reason to say, " What a fine country for the profession of the monarch " ?

Father Lobo relates that having had occasion to speak to the Emperor of Abyssinia, he asked to be allowed to see him. This request was immediately granted; but he had hardly entered, when he saw advancing towards him two tall chaps, who, without one word of explanation, began to beat him unmercifully. The astonished missionary shrieked with pain; but the men, one of whom held his arm, only struck the harder.

Suddenly a door opened, the prince appeared, and the two men ceased their belaboring.

"Why this cruel treatment?" cries the poor father, who was badly bruised.

"You have richly deserved it," is the answer; "when you pronounced the name of the emperor just now, you should have touched the ground with your hand. People must be taught to humble themselves when they speak the king's name."

We know that in Russia the knout is a great favorite. This punishment is less used now, but the stick proper has preserved all its rights. Lords, gentlemen, and masters, on the slightest pretext, have a perfect right to strike their subordinates. This bastinado is called battock. The slave or the peasant who receives it, after his punishment is over, kisses the hand and the knee of the one who has ordered it, and thanks him for not having ordered more.

17*

So in Sparta, in olden time, slaves were beaten as often as possible, in order that they might not forget their condition of servitude.

It is asserted that the terrible Mourawief was very expert in handling the cudgel. He was one day travelling alone in the environs of Moscow, and after riding several hours, he went down into a poor-looking *cabac*. The appearance of the inn-keeper accorded with his surroundings, and his face wore an eager, greedy expression. At sight of his guest's fine horse—a real son of Ukraine—his bump of acquisitiveness began to itch violently, and taking advantage of the moment when the vapors of the *rotchi* were cheering Mourawief's spirits, he said to him :

" I want your horse, my guest."

" Insolent dog ! " replied Mourawief, " do you want to steal my horse ? "

" No ; I want to buy him."

" You buy such a noble animal ? Well, yes ; I will sell him to you, but you must pay me the price that I shall demand."

" And how much is that ? "

" How much ? Thirty blows."

' Well, well, that is a queer price, but I am satisfied," replied the inn-keeper, who thought it the joke of an intoxicated man.

The next day he saddled his guest's horse, and brought him to him.

"That is your horse," said Mourawief.

"Mine!" exclaimed the inn-keeper, who had forgotten the occurrence of the day before.

".Yes; only you haven't paid for him yet; but you must now; so come, kneel; you owe me thirty blows."

"Have pity on me," said the inn-keeper, kneeling: "spare me ten blows; the club is so heavy."

"Well, I will spare you ten blows."

The inn-keeper burst into tears.

"Oh, spare me ten blows more—my poor wife, my children—"

"You have only ten to pay me now."

"Let it be five, I beg of you; you seem to have such a strong arm, and your eye frightens me."

"Well, five then—not one less; come, take your position."

The inn-keeper bent his back, and Mourawief, striking with his whole strength, counted:

"One, two, three, four—"

He raised his arm for the fifth, but threw his stick to the ground,. and quickly mounting his horse, said:

"I will give you the fifth when I return with my horse."

Among the Russian peasantry, when a young girl marries, her father, armed with a stick, asks her intended if he will take his daughter for his legitimate wife. If the answer is affirmative, the father requires his daughter to turn round three times, and gives her each time three blows on her shoulders, saying to her :

" My dear daughter, these are the last blows of fatherly tenderness that you will receive ; from this day I resign my authority to your husband." Then he presents the stick to the suitor, who out of politeness refuses, or rather pretends to refuse to take it.

" Your daughter will never need that chastisement," replies he gallantly. " I will never use it."

" At all events, take it," insists the father. " I made the same reply, but for all that I have often used it."

The husband then took it, the young wife made him a courtesey in token of submission, and the ceremony was ended.

Man is a creature of habit—and voluntary servitude, with him, as with animals, is the greatest proof we can have of the force of habit. Animals accustomed to the yoke bend to it willingly, and nations accustomed to slavery do not even try to know the advantages of liberty.

The bastinado is the principal punishment of criminals among the peasants of Livonia. These poor creatures allow themselves to be beaten without a murmur. In 1582, Stephen Barton, king of Poland, offered to deliver them from this tyranny, and to substitute light fines for the bastinado ; but the peasants would not listen to a proposition which would abolish their old custom, and they humbly entreated the king not to deprive them of the bastinado.

Here is another example of the force of habit :

When minister Saint Germain attempted to substitute whipping with the flat of a sword for the bastinado, the soldiers, who had become accustomed to the stick, were on the point of revolt, and he had to relinquish his innovation.

It would be hard work to up-root despotism in Russia. The millions of peasants who in this vast empire live under the rule of the stick, will probably never have sufficient energy to shake off the yoke of the lords and nobles. They will remain slaves of habit.

In America, the punishment of the stick is beginning to disappear with the slavery of the blacks.

Let us hope, then, that soon in no part of the world will the revolting spectacle be witnessed of human beings undergoing the punishment of brutes.

We, Frenchmen, in whom the ideas of liberty and equality seem innate, can hardly understand what a slave is, and we wonder how it is that one man can make thousands of them.

In order to make a man a slave, it is necessary to destroy in him every germ of intelligence. It is not enough to enthral his body; his mind must be stultified. In some states a man who taught his slaves to read and write, was severely punished. There are laws to protect animals, but none to protect slaves! The master even has a right to kill his slave, and the only safeguard of the latter is the cupidity of the former.

The negro having an intrinsic value, the white man would injure his own interests if he killed him, or inflicted punishments so severe as to interfere with his labor. So, to punish the slave without hurting himself, the master has chosen the stick, for the negro can return to his work after receiving the bastinado.

And so the great justiciary, so often the cause of death, may become a means of life.

CHAPTER IV.

SPIRITUAL AUTHORITY OF THE STICK.

*Clerical and abbatial flogging.—The illustrious flogged ones:
Godescale, Henry II., Louis VIII., Raymond VI.—Punishment
of Paul Olivarès for not believing in the torments of hell.—
Voluntary flagellation.—Fanaticism.— The flagellants.—Henry
III.— The rod in the convents.— The good shepherd uses his staff,
not to strike, but to guide his flock.*

N France, where the stick has always
been a sign of power, property, or pos-
session, the bastinado has left no traces ;
our laws have always dealt rigorously
with those who used the stick as a weapon.

Not so with religious laws. For ages all catholic
Europe was subjected to the spiritual authority of
the stick. The bishops had arrogated to themselves the right of using it on clergymen, and the
abbots on priors and monks. Even laymen were
not exempt from this correction, and the father
confessors administered it to them with rods
which the penitents themselves brought them for
that purpose. The theologians of the time declare
that nothing was more efficacious than clerical and

abbatial fustigation for the remission of sins and
the sanctification of souls.

In the tenth century very special canons exempt-
ed from abbatial fustigation monks, priests, and
deacons ; but for all that, in virtue of a judgment
rendered by Pope John XII., the monk Godescale
was formally flogged in the presence of Charles
the Bald and Bishop Otger.

In the thirteenth century it was decreed that
heretics especially should suffer this punishment.
This was before it had become the custom to burn
them alive.

Every one, rich or poor, noble or peasant, who
had disobeyed the laws of the church had to suffer
the bastinado.   This punishment was then so
common that it was used even at court.   So while
the feudal stick was performing feats of prowess on
the backs of serfs and peasants, the clerical stick
was exercising its spiritual and temporal authority
on those of lords, kings, and princes.   It was
justice.

From Saint Louis, who from a spirit of asceti-
cism allowed himself to be flogged by his confessors, down to Henry IV., who, after having ab-
jured received, publicly, at Rome, absolution, in
the shape of a flogging—on the shoulders of his
two ambassadors, Cardinals Duperron and d'Ossat

—how many princes, including Henry II., king of England, and Louis VIII., son of Philip Augustus, have like bigots and cowards bent to the spiritual authority of the stick!

Raymond VI., count of Toulouse, suspected of heresy, was publicly scourged with rods at the gate of St. Gilles at Valencia by order of the pope.

In the eighteenth century ecclesiastical authority still employed this means of conversion. It was in the tribunal of the holy Inquisition that the punishment of the stick was most used. It was often preceded by the confiscation of the penitent's property for the benefit of the Holy Office; and this was not the least of the motives for its frequent application.

We read in Bachaumont's Memoirs:

" On the 24th of November, 1778, the general tribunal of the Inquisition had a secret hearing, at which Paul Olivarès appeared, accused of heresy. Having been declared a heretic in all its forms, he presented himself in that character, holding in his hand a torch of green wax, and bearing the cross of St. Andrew.

" He was condemned:

" To the confiscation of all his property.

" To eight years of imprisonment in a monastery, during the first year of which he was to fast

18

on Friday, if his health permitted it, and this was to be decided by a spiritual director who would be appointed to fortify him in the practice of his religious duties, and to instruct him in the Christian religion.

"To say his prayers regularly morning and night, to read the reverend Father Grenade's 'Guide of Sinners,' and to recite every day, on his knees, the Rosary and the Creed.

"To forfeit all his titles and offices, and be declared forever disqualified from holding rank.

"Never in future to use garments of silk, velvet, gold or silver tissues, galloons and precious stones.

"Never to ride horseback or to carry arms.

"In his character of a heretic poor Olivarès had to make a solemn abjuration. He was absolved from the excommunication, and reconciled according to the rules prescribed by the holy canons.

"For that purpose four surpliced priests, each armed with a rod, presented themselves before the accused, whose bare shoulders received the spiritual flogging, while the psalm Miserere was being chanted by the assistant priests. He was then required to make his profession of faith. He was questioned on more than thirty articles of faith, but it seems that his answers did not satisfy the holy tribunal, for this terrible sentence was soon pronounced :

" ' We declare him duly convicted of heresy.'

" At these words, the poor man fell in his seat, weeping and moaning, *which augured well for his repentance.*"

The errors of Olivarès were indeed very grave, and well deserved the bastinado, confiscation, and the cloister. He had been convicted of not believing in the sixth commandment, the torments of hell, the punishment of purgatory, and—worse than all—of having been on friendly terms with Rousseau and Voltaire—we might as well say with the devil.

Religious laws which ought to be the most merciful, have long been the most inhuman ; and we find flagellation inscribed in the rules of nearly all the monasteries by their founders. The fathers of the church then firmly believed in the efficacy of the stick in religious life, and in the ninth century we find several great saints, Saint Dominique amongst others, setting the example of voluntary flagellation ; and from that time from east to west men scourged themselves for the love of God. Thousands of monks thus practiced on their own backs this ecclesiastical

punishment, which they afterwards applied so well
to the backs of unrepentant laymen. Religious
fanaticism soon knew no limits to this foolish
practice.

This mania gave rise to that sect of penitents
which became famous in the thirteenth century,
under the name of Flagellants; they used to flagellate themselves publicly.

One Ramier, a Dominican, moved by the misfortunes of Italy, thought that penance would
disarm the anger of God. The followers of this
monk marched in procession, stripped to the
waist, carried a cross in one hand, and a whip in
the other, and whipped themselves with so much
enthusiasm that the blood gushed from their
shoulders. Priests marched at their head, spoke
words of encouragement to them, and even set
them the example of flogging. This mania spread
all over Europe, but did not settle in France,
although the rod played its part there too, both
in public and private.

"In 1551," says the *Essais historiques sur Paris*,
"King Henry III., the chancellor, the courtiers,
and the ministers, were seen marching two by
two in the streets of Paris, dressed in long sacks,
with thick cords around their waists, and rods in
their hands to flagellate their shoulders."

In several of the cities of Provence, Avignon, Marseilles, Toulon, there are still numerous brotherhoods in whose institutions flagellation is obligatory. Those modern penitents still go in the streets with hoods on their heads, and cords round their waists, but they do not flagellate themselves in public. Instead of a rod they carry a wooden basin, and ask alms for prisoners. That is their way of honoring the Divinity.

The penitential stick has not yet quite disappeared from monastic usages—there are still human beings who, in the solitude of the cloister, bruise and tear their flesh with the sackcloth and rod. It is in women's convents that voluntary flagellation is most generally practiced.

I heartily pity those young women whom a sad fate has condemned to the cloister, and who in obedience to a barbarous rule, scourge themselves with the rod to expiate imaginary sins. We are not in the secrets of a contemplative life, but it seems to us that by these inhuman practices, these fanatical mutilations, God must be more outraged than honored.

Among the Pagans the priests used to lacerate their bodies to propitiate the gods.

Let us hope that, like the torture and the Inquisition, the superstitions and inhuman practices

18*

of the rod will disappear from all civilized countries.

To-day the laws of the church are no longer violent; are they any worse for it? Is the tolerance of our priests less efficacious. than the rigor of the priests of old?

It is by gentle means that they should endeavor to bring back into the fold the lost sheep. The good Shepherd uses the stick, not to strike, but to guide.

It is the same with teaching. Is instruction less diffused, more difficult to impart to-day, that in the colleges and schools the ferule and the whip are no longer used?

The whip! Another instrument of torture that shames humanity.

CHAPTER V.

THE WHIP.

How it was applied to the nobles.—The whip in England.—The cat-o'-nine-tails.—Judges with hanging clubs.

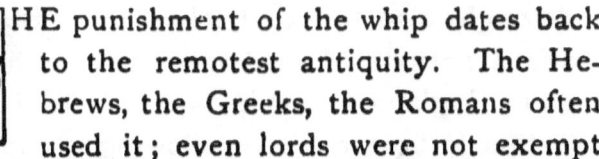HE punishment of the whip dates back to the remotest antiquity. The Hebrews, the Greeks, the Romans often used it; even lords were not exempt from it—but the great have always been privileged. Artaxerxas Longiminus ordered that only the *coats* of the nobles should be whipped.

The whip has always ruled, and still rules in Asia and Africa. Europe introduced it into America with the slave-trade, and it is there to-day that it is used with the greatest cruelty.

When, from the very beginning of society, we see how the rulers of the earth have vied with one another in inventing terrible punishments, we can not help wondering if there is any limit to the cruelty of man.

Of all punishments invented by human barbarity, that of the whip is the most odious, the most degrading; and yet it figures in the laws and the customs of every nation.   How many groans this frightful auxiliary of the stick has wrung, and still wrings, every day, from the negro and the serf!

There has been no whipping in France since 1789.   The Revolution which has abolished the stick, would not allow the use of the whip.   This punishment which France has stricken from her code ought also to be stricken from that of all civilized nations.   This is not the case, however; even in England the whip is still held in honor, or rather in horror.   The following is a feeble description of the torture as it is practiced to-day in London.

A half-naked man, with his hands tied, is fastened to the stake.

A sheriff and a physician stand by his side, and in front of him the executioner.   The doctor's business is to count the number of blows, and note the physical energy of the patient, and the sheriff's to make an official report of the punishment.

The executioner awaits the signal.   He holds in his hand a stick to which are attached nine leather straps, each one knotted at the end : this stick is called cat-o'-nine-tails.

Suddenly a piercing cry is heard—the poor convict has just received the first blow. The scene that follows is too horrible for words. Every blow—and they fall slowly and at equal intervals—tears away great lumps of flesh. The convict no longer cries—he howls. His strength soon fails, however, and the howl dies away on his lips—he moans feebly—a rattling sound is heard in his throat ; but the physician is there—he holds the patient's arm, feels his pulse, and when he sees that this panting, gasping human being is about to expire, he orders the executioner to stop.

The strongest man can not endure more than twenty-five blows of this terrible punishment.

England has always been partial to summary punishments, and the stick has always been one of the lawful instruments of torture. Edward the First created judges who carried *hanging sticks*, to punish violators of the public peace. These magistrates inflicted the punishment themselves upon those whom they had condemned to suffer it. It was unlawful for a judge to go out without having his stick hanging at his belt, and when he was hearing a case he held it in his hand.

CHAPTER VI.

THE LITERARY BASTINADO.

A law of Sylla.—Fear of the Stick.—The poet Roi and the Count de Clermont.—Beaumarchais among the Lazarists.—Let us thank the gods !

E have seen the stick, under different names and various forms, used through cruelty, folly, and superstition. We could also show how in social life it is the accomplice of private vengeance and animosity, or how it exerts its despotic authority under the shadow of the conjugal roof; but it would take up too much room, especially the chapter devoted to the flogging of women by their husbands ; for the part that the stick has played in marriage dates back to the beginning of society.

Next to women, poets and libellers have suffered most from the stick.

In all times and in all nations writers have been persecuted, and that is why history is so uncertain and obscure. " When we are not allowed to speak the truth," said Montesquieu, "we are always inclined to betray it." And that is what too often happened.

Sylla made a law punishing libellers and poets with death. Another king, whom Horace mentions in the second book of his epistles, said that whoever should dare to decry a Roman citizen should suffer the bastinado. "Whereupon our satirists," adds the flatterer of Augustus, "changed their style, and for fear of the stick they said no evil of any one, and wrote only agreeable verses."

This fear has perpetuated itself. After, as before the time of Horace, historians and poets were forced to become the flatterers of princes and lords for fear of becoming their victims.

Some of them, however, did not fear to expose their backs to the resentful stick, but boldly spoke the truth.

We have mentioned the case of Jean de Menny, who only avoided the bastinado by a witticism; while on the contrary it was a witticism which under the reign of Louis XIV. procured to the poet Roi this literary punishment. When the Count de Clermont was elected to the French Academy, the satirical Roi wrote the following lines:

> " Trente-neuf joints à zéro,
>   Si j'entends bien mon numéro,
>   N'ont jamais pu faire quarante :
>   D'où je conclus, troupe savante,
>   Qu'ayant à vos côtés admis
>   Clermont, cette masse pesante,
>   Ce digne cousin de Louis,
>   La place est encore vacante."

The poet paid for that bit of satire quite a respectable number of blows, which nearly cost him his life. If he had remembered that the Count de Clermont was a prince of the blood, and that this prince of the blood was also a prince of the church, and possessed several benefices which gave him the right to carry the abbatial stick, the unfortunate Roi would hardly have risked his epigram.

Beaumarchais did not escape the bastinado promised to poets by old Horace. Louis XV., who hated him for writing the " Marriage of Figaro," imprisoned him at St. Lazare, where the Lazarists were ordered to administer to him every morning a ration of rods. This mishap made him the hero of song and caricature; he was represented receiving the bastinado at the hands of a monk.

Mr. Victor Fournel in his book, *Du rôle des coups de bâton dans l'histoire littéraire*, also shows that the bastinado was a punishment inflicted on poets in the olden time. "So that," says he, "to treat a man like a poet meant to beat him with a stick." It was in the seventeenth and the eighteenth centuries that Mr. Fournel finds the victims of the *ultimo ratio* of the great personages of that time. He mentions no less than ninety names, Voltaire among them, who received the bastinado on the order of the Duke de Sully and at the hands of his servants. If the author had gone further back he would have found hundreds of them. " In the distribution of blows," said he, " the poets doubtless received the largest share, but they were by no means the only ones—without mentioning common people, archers and mechanics of all kinds, whose daily bread was the bastinado, it would be easy for us to prove that people of quality did not spare one another."

Let us thank the gods! The poets of to-day no longer fear the laws of a new Sylla against the freedom of the pen; they can arm themselves with the torches of the Furies and strike repeated blows, without having to fear the stick of a great lord or the rod of a Lazarist.

16

CHAPTER VII.

THE STICK OF THE THEATRE.

Harlequin's Stick.—Castigat ridendo mores.—Robert Macaire's Stick.—The Orchestra-leader's Stick.

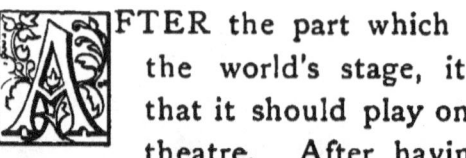FTER the part which it has played on the world's stage, it was quite just that it should play one on that of the theatre. After having served to fustigate the shoulders of the human race, it was used to fustigate its eccentricities—snatched from court and church, and placed resolutely in the hands of those reprobates " the sons of Belial "—as actors were then called. For it was to the theatre that hypocrites, bigots, and misers were summoned, with their vices and their follies, to be in their turn scourged with the stick.

It is the eternal law of retaliation, to which gentlemen, prelates, humble citizens, and financiers had to submit.

Our great Molière was the first to seize the stick and transfer it to the French stage. We well know what use he made of it, when he placed it in the hands of Scapin and Sganarelle.

About the same time, in the person of Domin-ique Biancolelli, the deobstruent wooden sword of Harlequin appeared on the stage of the Fair of St. Germain. It is from Italian comedy that this philosophic stick has come down to us, but it is to our poet Santenil that we owe the less philosophic *Castigat ridendo mores*, which is the epigraph to the life of the celebrated Italian actor.

This famous *Castigat ridendo mores*, which has become a proverb, so aptly recalls the idea of punishment attached to the stick, that we must allude to its origin.

One day Dominique, dressed in his theatrical costume, went to see Santeuil. With his wooden sword in his hand, his little hat on his ear, his girdle round his waist, and enveloped in his red cloak, he rapped at the door of Santeuil, who was writing.

" Who is there ? " asked the poet.

Dominique did not answer.

" Who is there ? " cried he again.

Still no answer.

" If you are the devil himself," exclaimed the poet impatiently, " come in."

Dominique took the hint, quickly threw back his red cloak, donned his mask and entered swag-geringly.

At sight of this strange looking personage, Santeuil appeared stupefied. The actor also aped astonishment, then jumped about making a thousand grimaces at him, and assuming the oddest postures, and also taking the liberty of using his stick.

Santeuil, angry, returned the blows with his fists, but Dominique knew how to evade them.

"I will know who you are, if you are the devil himself," exclaimed Santeuil angrier than ever.

"Who I am?" said Dominique.

"Yes."

"Well I am the Santeuil of Italian comedy."

"Ah, parbleu, if that is the case," replied the poet, "I am the Harlequin of the church of Saint Victor."

Dominique then raised his mask, and they embraced each other. The celebrated Harlequin had only called on Santeuil, to ask him to write a motto for his portrait. The poet wrote *Castigat ridendo mores;* and that, like the stick which inspired it, will go down to posterity.

Another stick of entirely French creation, and which made its *début* at the theatre with Frederick Lamaitre, is that of Robert Macaire. Who has not seen that stick, not at the theatre of the porte St. Martin, but at the Bourse, that other

HARLEQUIN'S STICK.

stage, where an indiscribable comedy is played every day ; who has not seen it, sometimes smiling, sometimes majestic, sometimes business-like, in the hand or under the arm of a true Robert Macaire, playing the part of knave with its inimitable postures.

Another theatrical stick which has never flogged any one, and yet has always known how to command obedience and respect, is that of the leader of the orchestra. It is the stick, or rather the sceptre that this absolute monarch is compelled to wield when he wants perfect harmony in his dominions.

For a long time, the leader's stick was a simple roll of paper at the theatres, but opera leaders used a real stick.

From Gambert, the first orchestra leader of our Academy of Music, who died in London in 1677, to George Hainl, who died June 5, 1873, twenty-two time-beaters have succeeded each other at the opera. Lulli was the first who used a real stick to lead the opera. Meyerbeer's stick was of massive gold.

19*

BOOK SIXTH.

THE CANE.

ONLY CHAPTER.

MONOGRAPHY OF THE CANE.

The cane in the eleventh century.—Under Louis XIV.—Civility and the cane.—Men of letters.—A lesson of wisdom.—What it is to be independent.—Celebrated canes.—Useful canes.—The electric cane.—Rich canes.—My cane.—The switch.—The proudest cane. —Equality before the cane.—The sceptre of France to-day.—M. Thiers' cane, and Marshal McMahon's truncheon.

I N a book devoted to the story of the stick, the cane, so called from the reed of which it is formed, deserves at least a chapter. It is pre-eminently the stick of equality. Every one has a right to carry it, ornamented and decorated according to his fancy. It is neither a sign of command, nor a mark of authority, nor an emblem of power; and if, in spite of its peaceable tendencies it sometimes strikes, it is because nothing on earth is perfect, not even the best of sticks.

The custom of carrying the cane began in the eleventh century, and ladies used to carry them then. We see in the *Chroniques de l'histoire de France*, that Queen Constance of Arles,* wife of King Robert carried one crowned with a bird. Ladies now only carry canes at the watering places.

The favor with which the cane is looked upon in all classes of society, seems to date from the time of Louis XIII. Men of the gown, the sword, and the court carried it then. It was at this time that the *sarbacane* made its appearance. This was rather a weapon than a simple stick, and on account of its hollowness was used by the beaux of Paris to send sugar-plums to ladies. This was their mode of warfare.

Under Louis XIV., canes were magnificently carved and ornamented with knobs and ravens'

---

* The cane that this queen carried ought rather to be called a stick; she used it less as an appendage to her costume, than as an instrument of cruelty. She was present in the church at the trial of her own confessor, Etienne, who was condemned to be burned alive as a heretic. Meeting him at the door of the tribunal, she put out his eyes with her stick—an act worthy of the feudal stick of the eleventh century, but these inhuman acts were then called *piety.*

beaks of gold. Colbert carried one of the latter
kind, which he never laid aside, not even in the
presence of the king. Louis XIV. tolerated this
breach of etiquette, and Colbert's example was
followed by his successors, to whom alone, however, it was permitted to enter the presence of
the king with a cane, provided that like that of
Colbert, the handle was a raven's beak of gold.

Under this reign, ceremony did not exclude
the cane, especially that with the knob of gold.
Charles Lebrun has represented the principal personages of the time, Villars, Crequy, Luxembourg,
Vauban, Catinat, and Turenne, with small ebony
canes.

Under Louis XV., the cane was much longer.
Lafayette, on his return from America, presented
himself at court with a very long one, and from
that time long ones became fashionable—they
were indispensable to a majestic walk and a grave
demeanor, and were the compulsory complement,
the neccessay accompaniment of the wig.

The revolution which had broken the feudal
and royal stick, soon shortened the cane, and
under the *Directoire* the *Incroyables* made their
appearance ; these were frightful twisted sticks,
which fashionable men twirled as they walked.

Modern civility does not permit the cane at

STICKS OF THE EIGHTEENTH CENTURY—THE AGE OF STICKS.

visits of ceremony. I consider the prohibition puerile, for I can not see how the carrying of this peaceful stick offends propriety, and I never without inward protest read these words at the doors of museums and other public places: "Gentlemen are requested to leave their canes in the vestibule." I can understand the exclusion of dogs—but not of canes—which for so many men have become more than a habit, a necessity.

No man who is not a born cane carrier, will ever learn to carry it gracefully ; but according to the manner in which he carries it, he will appear silly, intellectual, or consequential, and it even has the power of giving assurance to those who lack it. "When a man does not know what to do with his hands," said Méry to me one day, "he can put them on his cane." And surely this is better than thrusting them in his pockets.

Literary men are generally very partial to the cane ; I know some who never go out without a respectable rush in their hands ; but they do not arm themselves in this manner with belligerent intentions. With the exception of a few political fighters, who call themselves men of letters, because every morning they throw their unhealthy slaver into a large-sized journal, the writers of to-day are peaceable men, and if they sometimes make war among themselves, it is with their pens, and not with their canes.

"Why do you carry such a large stick with such good legs?" I one day asked one of my colleagues, who in the days of the ancient Greeks would gladly have become a disciple of Antisthenes.

"That," replied he, laughing, and exhibiting his stick, "is because I am afraid of dogs."

"I supposed it was to give yourself a stately air," I replied.

"A writer," said the philosopher, "being more prominently before the public than other men, should only be anxious to distinguish himself by the stateliness of his morals."

The cane had answered an impertinence by a lesson in wisdom.

A critic, well-known by a cane without which he never ventures into the street, said to me one day :

"Do you know why I always carry a cane?"

"Probably to enforce respect, in a very unliterary manner, for the rights of criticism."

"You are mistaken," replied he; "my bamboo, terrible as it looks, has never struck a single one of the enemies that my too truthful pen may have made, but it frightens them."

Putting the same question to a young author, whose severe-looking cane is hardly in keeping with his age and sprightly face, he replied:

"Oh, I carry a cane because it makes one look like an independent gentleman."

What a charming prospect! to be independent —a gentleman—it is the fond hope of so many literary men! But, my young friend, carrying a cane alone will not make you one. There are wealthy, independent men in literature as in commerce and industry, but remember that the faces of those who have made a fortune in literature have long paled, and their hands sweat over book and pen. No matter how intelligent you may be, never without work will fortune come to you except in the azure of your dreams. We are no longer in the times of easy life, when Jacob could go from Beersheba to Haran, in Messopotamia, with his stick in his hand, and his pocket empty.

The stick at that time represented activity— work. To-day the cane too often represents indolence—the *far niente*.

There is a cane, however, which still represents work, and which, thanks to the progress of civilization, is never transformed into a murderous weapon. It is the journeymen's cane. The cane is the distinctive badge of the journeymen. Certain societies of them have long ones, others shorter. The long ones with iron mountings are considered warlike.

In olden times workmen, journeymen of the different trades, especially in large cities, used to have bloody fights, and when they met they would cane each other unmercifully.

To-day the different societies of journeymen belong to a solidarity which is to unite all the workers of the earth.

The long and the short canes fraternize.

I have for a country neighbor an old marquis who has a passion for canes; he has made a collection of the most interesting of them, and among them are some very valuable ones. His collection includes all kinds, from the *sarbacane* of the exquisites of the court of Louis XIII., to that with the raven's beak used by the majestic personages of the court of Louis XIV.

The cane of the reign of Louis XV. is there by the side of the modern rattan. The marquis exhibits with delight those which—he says with deep conviction—have belonged to some celebrity.

One of these marvellous canes is thus labelled:

"Cane of Louis XIV. It is the one which the

great king threw out of the window to avoid striking Lauzun, when the latter, in the great gallery of Versailles, broke his sword before the king because Louis, having promised him the bâton of the grand master of artillery, had refused to give it to him.

"I will no longer serve a king who does not keep his word," Lauzun had said as he broke his sword.

"It shall not be said that I have struck a gentleman," the monarch had replied, as he threw away his stick.

"If the cane of Louis XIV. is apocryphal, the anecdote may be true," said I to the marquis one day, as he was showing me his collection.

"I," replied he, dryly, "doubt the anecdote, but the cane is authentic."

I saw that I had wounded my neighbor, and resolved to be more guarded.

"Here," said he, vivaciously, "look at this one —will you doubt again? I will show you its certificate of origin if you require it—it is the cane of Frederick II. of Prussia."

"This cane that of the great Frederick?"

"Yes, sir; read the label."

And I read:

"Cane of Frederick II. king of Prussia. It is the
20

one that his father, Frederick William, delighted to strike even ladies with when he walked on the streets of Berlin—it is the same with which this barbarous father twice struck, and nearly killed the grand prince who was one day to have the honor of counting Voltaire among his courtiers."

While I read, the marquis was opening a glass case where a number of canes with ravens' beaks were classed. He handed me one, on the label of which was:

"Voltaire's cane. It is the one which he held in his hand on the first day of April, 1778, the day when he was received triumphantly at the *Comedie Française*, and crowned by the Prince de Bauvan."

I examined several other celebrated canes. Each had its story, and I was very careful not to seem to doubt any of them ; I even praised them highly.

"Do not think," said he, "that in making this collection, curiosity has been my only guide. I have no special mania for canes—I am a philosopher. Pascal says, ' Man is a thinking reed '— well, all these canes are reeds. I see in them the men who have carried them, and I say to myself, these canes were a passive instrument in the hands of these men, as they were an instrument in the hands of the Creator."

"Has the marquis a bee in his bonnet," thought I.

"You do not know with what earnestness and passion I have sought for all these things, and what delightful hours they afford me. Nothing that man can leave behind him when he dies so well represents him as his cane. While during the course of his life, he so often changes his clothes, his carriages, his horses, his houses, and alas! even his friends, it is the same cane which always remains with him and sustains his last steps."

"It is true," murmured I.

"I will show you one of the most extraordinary, the most curious of them," said he enthusiastically, pleased at my assent. Saying which he pulled down from a shelf a rustic rod, on the label of which was written :

"This cane is one of those used by the Persian monks to brings to Europe the first eggs of the silkworm."

I uttered an "oh!" and thought to myself, "decidedly the marquis has a bee in his bonnet."

I shall not be surprised if some day he shows me, with the same tone of conviction, the cane with which Altken brought to Provence, in the sixth century, the first root of madder.

The cane is now used for various purposes; umbrellas, parasols, &c.; some are musical, and can be made to execute a double quickstep, and some can be used for seats. I am in earnest. The cane, which up to the present time has seemed principally intended to assist us in walking, can now be equally well used for a seat. By means of some ingenious mechanism it is only necessary to touch a spring, and the cane opens, extends, a piece of cloth is unrolled, and in an instant we have a perfect seat.

Of all the canes of modern invention the most extraordinary is that which a physician, a friend of mine, has just invented. It is a weapon of defense in the full meaning of the word—and absolutely benign, as every respectable weapon ought to be.

One night, on towards one o'clock in the morning, the physician and I were walking together arm-in-arm, when in the distance my friend perceived two men seated on a bench, and seemingly waiting for us.

"Those are perhaps two strollers," said he. "I am going to blind them so that they will not molest us."

I supposed he was joking; but it was no sooner said than done; a streak of light suddenly issued from the philosopher's cane, and struck the two men full in the face; they rose suddenly, trying to screen their dazzled eyes with their hands.

"They are two vagabonds," said my companion; "see their clubs."

Recovering from their first astonishment, the men walked away, muttering to themselves.

My friend's cane contained a galvanic battery, a small lamp with two burners, and a reflector with a short focus. On pressing a spring, a movable window opens, the battery works, and an electric light strikes the object to which it is directed, as a projectile would; it is a gun-cane, shooting an electric ray. At the distance of a hundred metres the electric cane will blind a man; it turns night into day wherever it directs its light.

It is from Africa, India, and the two Americas, that the reeds, rushes, rattans, and bamboos come, of which we manufacture our canes. Cane-making feeds several other industries, and the art has never before been brought to such perfection.

Canes are also manufactured from ebony, sharks' spines, varnished leather, twigs of palm, lemon and olive trees, and ebony wood.

The manufacturer may fashion these different twigs according to his own taste or caprice, as

20*

there is no longer any special form for the modern cane, the raven's beak having lost its prerogatives.

I saw at the Exposition of 1807 very graceful canes, elegantly mounted in gold, silver, and platina, in relief, with animals' heads, fawns' feet, entwined serpents, and set with rubies, turquoises, topazes, and amethysts. And as I looked at all these beautiful canes I thought of my own, which is only a modest rattan. But modest and simple as it is, I would not exchange it for the finest cane in the world; no, not even for one ornamented with diamonds. Why?

Because it was given to me by a poet friend one day, when I was about to set out on a journey, and these lines accompanied it:

> " Il existe un pieux usage
> Qui veut qu'à l'heure des adieux
> Deux amis se donnent un gage :
> Accepte ce rotin, et de ses triples nœuds
> Que notre amitié soit l'image."

By the side of the serious cane, we will place the flexible and merry switch.

Ladies carry it in the street, at the promenade, and at the races. How graceful it is, how free in all its movements ! It is rather vain, but never arrogant. It makes no pretensions to governing the world, nor to being a support—although it does sometimes assume the airs of a conqueror. The indispensable companion of a Don Juan, it is often as foppish. It is even a little provoking sometimes, but when we remember that it is the companion of merry youth, we can easily forgive it all its little faults.

The young man must have a switch just as soon as he leaves college ; later, when he has become grave, when youth has given place to manhood, he will abandon the switch for the cane.

Alas, my soul is sad ! The time for the cane has arrived, and the time will come when the cane must give way to the stick.

At twenty we carry a switch, at thirty a cane, and at sixty a stick. If at twenty we do not carry a switch, it is because we are predisposed to melancholy or to a precocious gravity ; and if at thirty we continue to carry it, it is because we have preserved a young and jovial disposition ; and if at sixty we promenade on the boulevard with a cane, instead of a stick, it is because we still think ourselves young and attractive enough to please.

There is another cane—the opposite of the switch—which has its place marked in this book. It is as stiff and rigid as the other is flexible : as grave and serious as the other is lively and cheerful; and yet, in spite of its severe name, it puts on an air of conquest, and tries to excite admiration. It is really a fine cane, and attracts attention by its magnificence and its pride.

It loves parade, pomp, display, splendor; it has a majestic presence, a superb bearing, a warlike aspect, and yet it is not a war-cane. It has never shed human blood, although it has often faced battles. Of yore it entered Berlin, Vienna, Moscow at the head of regiments, regulating the steps of the drummers, beating the march; and only lately it was seen impossible on the battle-field, commanding the bayonet charge.

This majestical cane, glorious above all others, the greatest of canes, is that of the drum-major.

One of the finest conquests of the revolution is equality before the cane. It is no longer used, as of old, to distinguish the gentleman from the common citizen; simple citizens and great lords carry it; it has become democratic—some say low—and yet it is more highly wrought, ornamented, and polished than ever.

Before 1789, the cane in the hand of a nobleman, was proud, haughty, insolent; always ready to strike the backs of citizens, who still humbly bend before its hereditary power. It had the stiffness, the arrogance, the impertinence of gesture, all the manners, all the habits of the feudal stick. It was the material tradition of the right of the strongest for which people had preserved all their old respect. But to-day the cane of the great lord is quite citizen-like; from arrogant it has become wheedling, and its feudal instincts have given place to affability.

The back of the plain citizen has straightened itself out to the height of that of the marquis; *small people* have grown; from nothing, they have become something, and those whom the nobles formerly had a right to cane on the slightest provocation, now take the liberty of caning in return.

So now the canes of the nobles, and those of private citizens are equal, and salute each other as they pass.

Pass on count, pass on baron, on the right sidewalk or the left one, with your eye-glass and your superb cane—here comes a man who has ennobled himself by his virtues, and has risen by his intelligence and work alone—like you, he carries a cane! Return his salutation, marquis—his cane came from the same factory as yours.

M. THIERS' CANE—MACMAHON'S TRUNCHEON.

For more than two years, a plain little cane of common origin has governed France—and this cane, small as it is, has signed a treaty of peace with a sceptre—the bloody sceptre of the despot of Germany.

On the 24th of May, 1873, a war stick succeeded to that peaceful cane. The sovereign power devolved on Marshal MacMahon.

May the stick borne by the new president of the Republic again raise up the immortal flag of France.

BOOK SEVENTH.

PROVERBS OF THE STICK.

DANS la bouche d'un fou il y a un bâton.
"In the mouth of the foolish is a rod.
This is a proverb of Solomon. Among the Arabians, stick is synonymous with punishment. Solomon meant that the foolish man carried in himself his own punishment.

"*Le blé est le bâton de l'homme.*" "Wheat is man's staff."
"I will break the staff of bread," says the psalmist, which means that to deprive man of bread is to deprive him of his stick.

"*La science est le bâton de la vie.*" "Knowledge is the staff of life."
This proverb needs no comment. Young man, who are yet in that happy age of the switch, when the time comes in which you will need a staff to

support your tottering steps, may you possess the knowledge that will sustain your soul

"*A vaillant homme court bâton.*" "A short stick for a brave man."

The meaning of this proverb is exactly the same as that of this other: "*A vaillant homme courte epée.*" "A short stick for a brave man." Mr. Querard thus explains it:

The Spartans, so renowned for their courage, had very short swords. One of them on being asked the reason of it replied: "It is to strike the enemy closer." The Roman sword which conquered the world was not much longer than that of the Spartans. This proverb was formerly used by the nobles, who alone had the privilege of carrying swords. Common men, whose arm was only a stick, said, "a short stick for a brave man." It is quite possible, however, that stick here meant sword, for the two words were formerly synonymous. Froissard, describing the battle of Poitiers, said that "blows with axes, swords, and other sticks of war were given and received."

"*Bon et mauvais cheval ont besoin d'éperon.*"
"*Bonne et mauvaise femme ont besoin de bâton.*"

" Good and bad horses need the spur." " Good and bad women need the rod."

Boccaccio attributes this proverb to the wise Solomon—but this voluptuous king was far too fond of the fair sex to be ungallant. He praises too poetically in many verses of his proverbs the " virtuous woman " to have ever wished to have " good " women flogged.

" It is better to dwell in a wilderness than with a contentious and angry woman," also says this Sage in his book of proverbs. It is this " bad " woman who now, as she formerly did, needs the stick.

" *Pendant que le bâton va et vient les épaules se reposent.*"—" The shoulders have a rest between blows."

This proverb is used figuratively, sometimes ironically, to depict the unhappy situation of a man continually exposed to the reiterated strokes of bad fortune—sometimes seriously, meaning that there is no pain so persistent but has some slight intermission. The same proverb is used by the Portuguese : " *Em quanto o pao cai i vom, folgao as costas.*" They use it in a moral sense, and mean that we should never despair, and that God chastises those whom he wishes to bring back to him.

21

" *Bâton porte paix.*"—" The stick brings peace."
A man who is in a condition to defend himself is not attacked ; we are compelled to live in peace with an armed man.   In many countries the stick is vulgarly called *justice of the peace.*

" *Bâton porte paix et faquin faix.*"

This is a threat addressed to boors and blunderers, intimating that they will be made to keep the peace by being treated like *faquins,* that is to say, be made to bear a heavy load of blows on the shoulders.   The word *faquin* formerly signified street porter.   It must be added to the list of words that have degenerated, for it now only means a presumptuous, impertinent little dandy, with no merit whatever; a ridiculous and insignificant being for whom Roqueplan has invented this typical word : " *petit crevé.*"

" *Etre reduit au bâton blanc.*"—" To be reduced to the white stick."
It is said that this expression is an allusion to the ancient custom of soldiers who had capitulated leaving the garrison with a stick in their hands, that is, with only the wooden part of the lance.   But this is certainly a mistake, for this custom was only introduced because the stick

without its bark was a sign of poverty and subjection, affected particularly by beggars and prisoners.

We know that according to the terms of the
Salic law, the murderer compelled to leave the
country, when he could not pay the composition,
left the house with nothing on but his shirt, un-
girdled, bare-footed, and a stick in his hand *palo
in mano.*

" I do not pity boys," said Luther ; " they can
live anywhere if they know how to work: but the
poor little world of girls has to seek a living with
a white stick in its hand."

" *Le tour du bâton.*"

The casual and often illicit profits of an office.
This expression, according to Borel, comes from
two words, *bas* and *ton* (low and tone), because
being used to make an unjust profit, it is said in
a low tone—*d'un bas ton* in the ear of the person
interested.

> " Quand on y fait un bail de quoi que ce puisse être
> Et qu'on a dit tout haut ce qu'on en offre au maître,
> On prend un ton plus bas pour le revenant bon,
> Et voilà ce que c'est que le *tour du bâton.*"

" *Faire sauter a quelqu'un le bâton.*"—"To
make any one pump the stick."

This is an allusion to that amusement of shepherds, who, in driving their flocks in and out of
the fold, placed themselves at the entrance with
their crooks horizontally raised to a certain
height, to have the pleasure of seeing their sheep
jump over them.   Le Laboureur in his *Discours
sur l'usage des armes*, said that it may have an
historical origin, which he dates back to the primitive use of the saltier, which he says was an instrument for exercise before it became an armorial
ensign, known as "Saint Andrew's cross."

"*A vilain ne mets pas le bâton en main.*"—"Do
not invest the villain with a stick."

This proverb means that authority and power,
of which the stick is the symbol, should never be
given to the ignorant, because they are apt to
forget themselves and become insolent when they
are in power.

Aristotle advised Alexander never to invest
with authority those whom nature had made to
obey; and it is probably this wise advice which
suggested the proverb.

Claudian has said in his invectives against Eu-
tropius, that no one shows less mercy than a
blackguard raised above his condition. *Asperius
nihil est humili cum surgit in altum.*

To-day the dreaded blackguard is the rich *parvenu.* He thinks riches can take the place of education, but finding that well-bred people ignore him, he revenges himself for their scorn by ruling his servants with a rod of iron.

"*Commander à la baguette.*"—"To rule with a hard hand "—or " To rule with a rod of iron."

That is, to command in a hard and haughty manner.

"*Etre servi à la baguette,*" means to be served with respect and promptness. Some authors see in this expression an allusion to the magic wand; others think, with more reason, that it has reference to the rod which was given as a token of authority to civil and military chiefs.

"*Il crie comme un avengle qui a perdu son bâton.*" " He cries like a blind man who has lost his stick."

That is, he has lost what he most needed. The corollary of this proverb is: a druggist without sugar; a banker without money; a merchant without credit—they are alll blind men, who have lost their sticks, that is, they are in need of the thing which is most needful to their profession.

21*

The stick has given us several other proverbs: " *Il faut s'assurer de son baton.*"—" Make sure of your stick "—that is, of the means which are to make your enterprise successful. " *N'avoir ni baton ni verge.*"—" To have neither stick nor rod " —that is, to be without defense, protection, or support. The word stick for support enters into the composition of many other phrases of the same kind. To find in one's son the staff of one's old age, etc.

" MARTIN—BATON."

It used to be the custom to give the names of saints to animals, and the ass, it was said, was named Martin. But why Martin for the ass? Perhaps in allusion to the word *mart*, which is the root of several words which designate objects used to strike, or which express the action of striking, like *marteau* (hammer), *marteler* (to hammer), *martient* (tilt hammer), etc. *Martin Baton* seems naturally to come from that, and means the stick of Martin, or the stick which drives Martin. It is probable that the name of Martin was only given to the ass, because this useful animal generally receives a very liberal supply of blows with a stick.

Rabelais puts these words into the mouth of Panurge: "I will beat her if she angers me— *Martin Baton* shall do his work."

And this fable:

Martin Baton accourt l'âne change de ton ; Ainsi finit la comédie.

The synonym of *Martin* and *Baton* in familiar language is very old. Joan of Arc swore by her *Martin*, that is, by her stick.

"*Ce sont des bâtons flottants.*"—"They are floating sticks."

That is said of persons and things which, seen at a distance, seem very important, but which on close examination are found not to be so.

It is an allusion to that fable of Esop, of travelers perceiving in the distance, on the sea, something which at first seems to be a vessel, then a bark, and finally nothing but a twig of grape-vine, which the waves send toward them.

How many admirable things might upon examination be justly assimilated to these floating sticks. How many things there are, to which this line might be applied: "*De loin c'est quelquechose et de près ce n'est rien.*"

"*Tirer au bâton avec quelqu'un.*"

This expression is used in speaking of a person in discussion with another person of less consequence concerning a pre-eminence or some advantage which the latter disputes with the former. We say, *tirer au bâton*, to dispute the authority of which the stick is the symbol.

" *Tirer au-courts bâtons*," was formerly said of " *tirer à la courte-paille*,"—" to draw the short straw." The game of the short straw (*courtepaille*), refers to the custom of cutting in two equal pieces a bit of wood or straw, a symbol of investiture, to put these together again, and produce them if necessary as witnesses.

" *Faire une chose a bâtons-rompus*." This expression is a metaphor taken from the beating of a drum, which consists in using the drum-sticks alternately and at intervals; it is called *rompre les bâtons*, and is the reverse of *aller rondement*

" *Mettre des bâtons dans les roues*."—" To put a spoke in his wheel."

Before the invention of the shoe and the drag, sticks were used to stop the wheels of carts; so to put a stick in one's wheel, is to interfere with his progress, to prevent him from getting along.

It is very seldom that the unsuccessful man does not say some one has put a stick in his wheel.

How many are there who loiter by the wayside, and by their listlessness, their unfitness, their improvidence, have put sticks in their own wheels, and then accused others of having done it for them.

This proverb is current, especially among literary men. If a play has been refused at the theatre, a *feuilleton* at the newspaper office, or a book at the publisher's, the author instantly imagines himself a victim of jealousy, and declares that some one has put a stick in his wheel. He does not, perhaps, suspect that his play is impossible, his *feuilleton* wearisome, and his book vulgar.

Ah, my young friend, are you sure that your work is perfect, and that it was not refused in order to give you an opportunity to do better?

Read this anecdote concerning me.

I was about twenty. I had just written my first book, and the happy thought occurred to me of submitting my manuscript to one of our most learned critics, who was editor-in-chief of a review.

Of course I thought my work perfect.

"I promise to read your manuscript within a week," said the chief.

A week later I was in the sanctum. I saw my work on the desk, and I saw that he had read it.

" Are you courageous?" said he to me, suddenly.

" Perhaps so," stammered I, astonished at this brusque question.

" Are you industrious?"

" I think so."

" Well, I have read your work, and there is some good in it, but you can do better. Would you have the courage to write it over again without reading it?"

I fell from the seventh heaven.

" If you advise me to do it."

" I not only advise, but I urge you to do it."

With these words, he returned me my manuscript, saying:

" Bring it back rewritten, but do not read it."

" To show you that I will follow your advice, here it is," said I.

And I heroically threw my manuscript into the the fire, at which he seemed much pleased.

" Very well," said he, smiling.

He gave me some instructions, and I went away—rather sad, but not discouraged.

Three months later my rewritten work was published in the review, and afterwards in a book.

I never recall to mind the first step in my literary career, without coming to the conclusion, that many of those who think some one has put a stick in their wheels, would have succeeded if they had not forgotten this other proverb: " Be sure of your stick."

" *Ne touchez pas au bâton.*"—" Do not touch the stick."

This proverb originated in the custom which still exists—especially among children—of placing a small stick on the shoulder, and saying, " Touch this stick if you dare ; if you do, I will strike."

There are many other proverbs about the stick —this one for instance : " An author without wit, and a manufacturer without money, are two blind men who have *lost their sticks.*"

It is said of a man who appears embarrassed or does not know how to behave, that he has lost his stick.

Making useless efforts to succeed in an undertaking, or speaking without being understood or believed, is called beating the water with a stick.

I hope that I, dear readers, in writing this little book, have not *beaten the water with a stick.*

LAST CHAPTER.

THE CIVILIZING STICK.

HAVE one more stick to speak of—one which in all times has enjoyed an undisputed authority, a dreadful power, the mightiness of which is still increasing. It governs neither by arbitrariness nor by violence—but by reason. If it often makes its enemies tremble, it never overpowers them, and it never, like so many despotic sticks, imposes its law by the right of the strongest—*argumentatum baculinum*—but by the right of the most just.

Sticks were worshipped in ancient times—but this one more than all others has deserved altars, for it has said *Fiat lux* to the immaterial world, as God had said it to the physical world. It is through its agency that the light of intelligence has spread through the world, that eternal truths have been received, and that civilization will one day spread its wings over all the nations of the earth.

But what is this light-bearer—this civilizing stick? It is the pen.

The part that the stick has played in the art of writing is very great. The first pens were simple sticks or cane-stems, called *calam*, and our first books were written on the barks of trees, or pieces of wood. So both book and pen originate with the stick.

In most languages the book obtains its name from the tree, or that part of it which originally furnished the material for writing upon. *Buch* in German signifies both *beech* and *book*. And what shows that this double meaning is not accidental, is that *buch-staben* signifies letters; *staben* is derived from *stab*, a stick. This reminds us that the Teutons and Germans traced their characters on beech chips, as the Chinese did on the bamboo.

Not only was the stick the first instrument which was used by man to transmit his thoughts and write books, but without it the books of our forefathers would never have reached us.

We know that most of the manuscripts of antiquity were volumes in the true sense of the word, *a volere;* that is to say, they were composed of leaves placed one upon the other, written only on one side, and rolled on sticks. So our first libraries were composed of sticks, and the instrument used in writing the book served also to preserve it.

22

We also know that dispatches, messages, and even private letters were written on the bark of trees, and rolled on sticks.

The stick is therefore seen to have served as an instrument to write the thoughts of men to preserve them, and to transmit them.

Have we not good reasons for calling it the civilizing stick?

It was not until the seventh century that the stick was superseded by the quill. But as if it had been decreed by God that this instrument should be in all things the best and the worst, we see, in our age of iron, the stick which holds the metallic pen dethrone the quill.

www.ingramcontent.com/pod-product-compliance
Lightning Source LLC
Chambersburg PA
CBHW031344070726
47496CB00017B/1647